WRITING FANTASY FICTION

Sarah LeFanu

A & C Black · London

First published 1996
A & C Black (Publishers) Limited
35 Bedford Row, London WC1R 4JH

ISBN 0-7136-4260-2

© 1996 Sarah LeFanu

A Story Must be Held
Reprinted by permission of Curtis Brown Ltd
Copyright © 1990 by Jane Yolen
First appeared in *COLOURS OF A NEW DAY: WRITING FOR SOUTH AFRICA*
published by Lawrence & Wishart

A CIP catalogue for this book
is available from the British Library.

Typeset in 11/12pt Palatino
Printed in Great Britain by Redwood Books, Trowbridge, Wilts

Contents

Books in the 'Writing' series
Freelance Writing for Newspapers by Jill Dick
The Writer's Right by Michael Legat
Writing for Children by Margaret Clark
Writing Crime Fiction by H.R.F. Keating
Writing Erotic Fiction by Derek Parker
Writing Fantasy Fiction by Sarah LeFanu
Writing about Food by Jenny Linford
Writing Historical Fiction by Rhona Martin
Writing for Magazines by Jill Dick
Writing a Play by Steve Gooch
Writing Popular Fiction by Rona Randall
Writing for Radio by Rosemary Horstmann
Writing for the Teenage Market by Ann de Gale
Writing for Television by Gerald Kelsey
Writing a Thriller by André Jute
Writing about Travel by Morag Campbell

Other books for Writers
Writers' and Artists' Yearbook
Word Power: a guide to creative wiriting by Julian Birkett
Research for Writers by Ann Hoffmann
Interviewing Techniques for Writers and Researchers
by Susan Dunne

Preface

While I have been writing this book it has become clear to me that during the course of it I have been attempting to answer a series of questions that were in my mind, unconsciously perhaps, about fantasy.

Why is fantasy important? Why do we need fantasy? What is fantasy? Where are its roots, and how far do its branches reach?

However, this is a practical book. I hope that it will encourage you and corroborate your desire to write fantasy by exploring some of its many manifestations. This book will not teach you how to write. There is only one person who can teach you how to write: yourself. But you can draw on all sorts of help along the way, especially in the work of other writers, and the aim of this book is to explore what you can learn from different sources about writing fantasy, and to point out what you may find helpful.

What I hope to do is to suggest some practical answers to some practical questions. I may not be able to provide all the answers, but by raising the questions I would hope that you, writer or aspiring writer of fantasy, might find your own answers.

Ask yourself: why do I want to write fantasy? what is the kind of fantasy that I want to write? how am I going to set about writing fantasy? when am I going to start? how am I going to get published?

Let's look at that first question now and eliminate one reason for writing fantasy. The assumption of this book is that you are writing fantasy for some other reason than that you want to become very rich and successful. If you want to become very rich and successful you should not be writing fantasy. If you want to become very rich and successful you should not be writing. You should be studying law or taking your accountancy exams.

The question, why fantasy?, will run throughout the book. The question, what kind of fantasy?, will be addressed in a general way in chapter 1, and will continue in chapters 2, 3 and 4, which will also look at the 'how'? In those chapters I will be looking at how a range of fantasy writers build and develop their worlds, in other words, how they write. Chapters 6, 7 and 8 address the specifics of fantasy for children, dark fantasy and comic fantasy. When are you going to start? This has a very simple answer: now. The problems and difficulties surrounding that simple statement are addressed in chapter 5, which also deals further with the process of 'how'. This is the nitty gritty: the transformation of images and ideas into language. How do you communicate your world to your readers?

Why, what, when and how? Whatever the answers are that you find for yourself, I hope very much that by reading this book you will be encouraged and fortified. This last may seem a strong word to use in the circumstances, but I believe that writing is arduous and can only be achieved by the strong-hearted.

I also believe that anyone who wants to write fantasy – and this must mean you, gentle reader – probably has an inkling already of both the difficulties and the rewards that await them. I am not, of course, talking about material rewards (we leave those to the lawyers and accountants).

Why you, dear reader, want to write fantasy must be, I think, intimately bound up with the question I found myself asking throughout the writing of this book: why is fantasy important?

One of our great contemporary writers of fantasy, and one to whom I will refer you again at certain points in this book, has offered an answer to these questions. Here is Ursula K. Le Guin:

> It is by such statements as, 'Once upon a time there was a dragon,'
> or 'In a hole in the ground there lived a hobbit' – it is by such
> beautiful non-facts that we fantastic human beings may arrive, in
> our peculiar fashion, at the truth. ('Why Are Americans Afraid of
> Dragons?' in *The Language of the Night*, p.36)

I hope that by exploring just a little the roots and branches of fantasy, and by letting some of these wider questions lurk darkly on the edges of the page, you will find in this book not just the practical help that every beginning writer needs, but also something to build up and sustain your own faith in your enterprise.

1
What is fantasy?

Nobody has come up with a hard and fast definition of fantasy, and I am not going to try here. Fantasy is too all-encompassing. But we can think about the tendencies you find in fantasy, and we can think about some of the things that fantasy includes. Fantasy concerns itself with the unexplained and the unexplainable. It treats with magic and with mystery, and sometimes with the supernatural. Very often a fantasy story has a secret at the heart of it. The story may be to do with uncovering that secret. And while a mystery may be unravelled, it does not necessarily have to be explained. In the same way, magic does not have to be explained. In fact, it cannot be explained. In a fantasy world, it just is. Very often, you will find, it is the relation of the characters to the magic in a fantasy world that forms the basis of the plot. For, in fantasy, the magic is the source of knowledge and of power. It can be used and abused, it can be sought and found, it can be chased after and lost, it can be avoided and fled from, but it is there, centrally. To say that magic cannot be explained is not to say that it has no rules. 'Just because "anything goes" in fantasy, as opposed to in the realist novel,' says the writer Lisa Tuttle, 'does not mean that *everything* goes.' You will find that fantasy writers take liberties with the laws of this world, and then replace them with other laws which define the workings of the magic in the worlds they have created.

The background to a fantasy story is often based on a period in past history, very often with feudal or indeed quasi-mediaeval elements. You are likely to find social hierarchies: priestly ones, or courtly ones. There are many kings and queens, princesses and princes; sometimes scholars and philosophers; beggars, knaves, conmen and whores. You will not, on the whole, find democracies. But you will find heroes: women and men, or creatures who are neither but are nonetheless courageous, clever, generous and wise.

What else might you find in a fantasy world? You might find elves or orcs, dragons or unicorns, you might find fiends and fairies, you might find hobbits, or rabbits, or talking pigs ... You will probably, although not definitely, find some humans. You will definitely find emotion, drama, adventure; you will find love, desire, hate, treachery, sacrifice, self-sacrifice; you will find good and evil and the battle between the two.

Fantasy and science fiction

Throughout this book I will be directing your attention to a variety of writers of fantasy and using parts of their work to exemplify or illumine different aspects of fantasy writing. Many of these writers are known as writers of science fiction as well as of fantasy; in the anthologies and magazines to which I refer, you will see that the two forms often sit happily side by side, and indeed intermingle. The reader of this book will almost certainly be a reader of fantasy, and the chances are extremely high that she, or he, will also read science fiction, even if it is only the science fiction that is written by favourite fantasy writers.

Some critics have attempted to draw a line between the two forms. I think it is more useful, if we are thinking in terms of what fantasy includes, and of what you, the writer, can include in your fantasy, to see it in terms of cross-fertilisation rather than separation. Peter Nicholls gives what I think is a very apt example of two books that may well appeal to the same readers, showing how closely related fantasy and science fiction can be: 'Although the world of Tolkien's *The Lord of the Rings* (1954–5) allows magic, where that of Herbert's *Dune* (1965) does not, the two books have in common the creation of an immensely detailed, richly imagined alternate world in which individual heroism can play an important role.' (*The Encyclopedia of Science Fiction*, p.211)

In order for your created world to work, whether it is or is not a world that has magic as one of its defining properties, then it must indeed be 'immensely detailed' and 'richly imagined'. We shall be looking at ways of achieving this through-out the course of this book. But first let's look more closely at what makes people want to be enticed into fantasy worlds. What makes them want to lose themselves in a world that is very different from their own? In other words, what makes them want to read fantasy? And from the point of view of the writers, where on (or off) earth do they find those fantasy worlds?

Reading fantasy

There is no question that many people read fantasy, and that many people write it. Fantasy is enormously popular. Although I have just been talking about the cross-fertilisation of fantasy and science fiction, in terms of sales it is fantasy novels – the ones that include the magic and the kings and queens and the battles between good and evil – that are up there at the top. Fantasy plays a large part in contemporary films and, more recently, has been providing world after world in interactive computer games. (Here's another interesting cross-fertilisation: the proliferation of fantasy worlds within the science fictional world of cyberspace.) So while there are as many fantasy worlds as there are writers to invent them, there are obviously some common aspects of them – themes, or landscapes, or characters, or stories, – that have a very wide appeal.

Why, then, do so many people read fantasy? And why should they read yours instead of, or as well as, the work of other writers they know and love?

Is it simply that they have a thing about dragons, and prefer to read about them than about urban violence, crack dealers, broken marriages in shire villages, or career women whose lives revolve around sex'n'shopping? Probably not. Think about some of the fantasy you have read recently. All right, on the whole it is non-urban, but it is as full of violence as any non-fantasy fiction. Possibly it is even more violent because of the scope it allows for large scale warfare. Now, there is a clue: fantasy worlds tend to be less populated than our own world (and of course it is in science fiction that we find overpopulation as a recurrent theme, not just for the exploration of the breakdown of social structures, but for the leap into outer space and in more recent science fiction, into cyberspace). You may not find crack dealers, but you will find peddlers of dreams, bright ones as well as dark ones. Broken marriages in the shires? You maybe won't find the vicars trying to offer good advice, but you will find relationships foundering, and unrequited as well as requited love. You won't find shopping, but you will most certainly find sex. Drugs, sex, violence, passion, despair ...

Yes, they are all there, they are centre stage. You might say that in fantasy you are turning from all that is not intense, towards intensity, heightened emotion, life – and death – on a grand scale.

People read fantasy because it is not a depiction of the everyday modern world in which they live. It offers a picture of another world and another time. This is not to say that the fantasy world and the fantasy time are not related to our own world and our own time. However, it is what you might call the 'otherness' of fantasy, its difference from the everyday world, that constitutes a great part of its appeal.

There is a great deal of clutter in the modern world we live in. Our world is full of other people and it is in our negotiations with other people, whether it is in the supermarket, or on the internet, that we have to pick our way through all that clutter. The clutter, or paraphernalia of the modern world includes mortgage repayments, council tax, motorway traffic jams, waiting for crowded public transport; it includes supermarket shopping, the school run, the crowded ferry, the queue in the post office; it includes houses, roads, shopping centres.

Fantasy worlds have mountains, rivers, plains, deserts ...

So, where are they? How do you get to them?

Finding a fantasy world

Ursula Le Guin describes pulling a strange old book called *A Dreamer's Tales* off her father's bookshelf when she was twelve years old and reading:

> Toldees, Mondath, Arizim, these are the Inner Lands, the lands
> whose sentinels upon their borders do not behold the sea.
> Beyond them to the east there lies a desert, for ever untroubled
> by man: all yellow it is, and spotted with shadows of stones,
> and Death is in it, like a leopard lying in the sun. To the south
> they are bounded by magic, to the west by a mountain.

From Toldees, Mondath, Arizim, the Inner Lands described by Lord Dunsany in *A Dreamer's Tales*, through the snowy landscapes of Narnia, including the archipelago of Ursula Le Guin's Earthsea, to the echoing corridors of Mervyn Peake's

Gormenghast, the forests and lakes of Marion Zimmer Bradley's Avalon and the mountains, villages and city streets of Terry Pratchett's Discworld; none of these places exists out there. They are all Inner Lands. They are the landscapes of the imagination. And, Ursula Le Guin goes on to say, 'I was headed towards the Inner Lands before I ever heard of them.' ('A Citizen of Mondath', in *The Language of the Night*, p.20)

Some imaginary lands from legend and literature are so much a part of our culture that they seem to have a real existence. You may well know as much about El Dorado as you do about some place that you have heard of but never visited, such as the Kolyma region of Siberia, or the high Andes, or even the Basque country or the Loire valley. What about Shangri-La, or the lost world of Atlantis, Ruritania, The Isles of the Blest, Lyonesse, Cockaigne, Middle-Earth?

These worlds are so much a part of our heritage that you probably don't know who first invented them. You may know Middle-Earth, the land of hobbits, orcs, trolls and dwarves invented by J.R.R. Tolkien. But the others? Some come from legend and folktale and so are part of an oral tradition that has no single author. But single authors might have borrowed them to use in their own works. Take Lyonesse, for instance, or Lyones, which is traditionally meant to be an area of land that stretched from Land's End at the tip of Cornwall out to the Scilly Isles, and was long ago submerged beneath the waves. Malory, in *Le Morte D'Arthur*, the first prose telling in English of the tales of King Arthur and his court, has Lyonesse as the place where Tristram comes from (he is known as Tristram de Lyones); in Tennyson's poem *Morte d'Arthur*, published some four hundred years later, Lyonesse is the place where the last battle between Arthur and Mordred takes place; and, one hundred and fifty or so years after that, Lyonesse is one of the outlying lands, Cockaigne being another one, in which wars and skirmishes are being waged in the American fantasy writer Michael Swanwick's *The Iron Dragon's Daughter*.

These worlds have such resonance that it can almost be forgotten that they are fantasy worlds. It is because their existence is so much a part of our imaginative and literary thinking that writers can borrow them and refashion them. Legend, myth and folktale constantly feed into contemporary literature, and perhaps nowhere more directly than into fantasy.

Some lands of course are very much associated with a single author, and although they may not be confused with 'real' lands in the way that Lyonesse or Avalon can be, they are nonetheless so much a part of our thinking that they carry a reality of their own. I would give Jonathan Swift's Lilliput as an example of this (and the other lands that Gulliver visits on his travels: Brobdingnag, Laputa and the land of the Houyhnhnms and the Yahoos), and Frank Baum's Oz. This is at least partly to do with the proliferation of the ways of representing these lands: Swift's work has been repackaged so many times that you may have come across it as an illustrated children's book rather than as a devastating satirical picture of the British at politics and play and of the foibles of the human race in general. And like Oz it has appeared in comic strips, in film, on television, in songs and in other people's books. 'Yahoo' (but not the too-good-to-be-true and almost unpronounceable Houyhnhnm) has become a descriptive word in English. You certainly don't have to have read the original books in which these worlds appear to know all about them and what you will find there.

It is perhaps worth remembering how many of the fantasy worlds that you are familiar with are represented as lost worlds. H. Rider Haggard found one in *King Solomon's Mines*; Arthur Conan Doyle in *The Lost World*; Edgar Rice Burroughs in *The Land that Time Forgot*; storytellers past and present have found a world in Avalon, Michael Crichton and Stephen Spielberg – film-makers have to be numbered amongst our modern storytellers – in *Jurassic Park*.

So perhaps you do not have to create a world. What you have to do is find a world, to rediscover a world that exists but has been lost. And then depict it so that others can enter into it with you. And where will you find it? Not out there, although you will be incorporating knowledge and experience from out there, but from inside, from your own Inner Lands.

Writing is not an easy task. Writing fantasy is perhaps particularly hard because you are striving to represent, in a convincing credible way, something that, until it is on the page, only you can see. It is important to remember, and I will stress it throughout this book, that there are no hard and fast rules, that the blank page, although it may be frightening as you sit in front of it, is also exhilarating, because it is yours.

On this page you will create your world. You are striving to put on the page and to show your readers the mountains, deserts, rivers and oceans of your own heart. Not an easy task, but one that is enormously worth doing.

In the next chapter we will look at how you set about creating a fantasy world, building it up and mapping it for your readers. But first let us look briefly at some classic fantasy writers of the past, and at some recent and contemporary writers, to see what are the themes, the characters, the landscapes and the stories that we find in their work. These are the writers that people have read and are reading. What do they offer? What is their appeal? What do their fantasy worlds encompass?

Classic fantasies

Let's look briefly at some classic fantasies. From the nineteenth century: Charles Kingsley's *The Water-Babies: A Fairy Tale for a Land-Baby* (published 1863). Tom flees from the real world of cruel employers and rigid social distinction and falls into an underwater world where he is transformed into a water-baby. Life underwater is wonderfully realised: Kingsley had a keen interest in marine and seashore life, as well as being a passionate social reformer. Both aspects are there in his created world. Although the story has strong moral elements, it does not read like a moral tract – the underwater world is too imaginatively depicted for that.

Lewis Carroll's *Alice's Adventures in Wonderland* (1865) (followed by *Through the Looking Glass*): it has been suggested that the enormous popularity of the Alice books is partly at least to do with the fact that Lewis Carroll was not preaching any morality in them (unlike *The Water-Babies* just mentioned). Alice falls down a rabbit hole into an underground world of talking, riddling, crazy creatures which is all held together by an extraordinary logic of its own.

Both these novels could be described as 'cross-over' novels: someone from the 'real' world falls into another world (taking the reader with them). In the nineteenth century a rationale was conventionally called for: Tom's crossover is into death, Alice's is into sleep and dreams.

In Frank L. Baum's *The Wizard of Oz* (1900) Dorothy is swept away from her home in Kansas by a tornado and set down in an otherworld of witches, lions, scarecrows and tin men without hearts. The yellow brick road leads Dorothy and her companions to self discovery.

Edgar Rice Burroughs' *Tarzan of the Apes* was published in 1914, and during the next fifty years another twenty or so novels followed (including *The Son of Tarzan, The Tarzan Twins, Tarzan and the Ant Men*). Enormously popular, these stories explore the human/nature interface through adventure, excitement and derring-do.

Moving on a bit, we come to C.S. Lewis's *Narnia* books, which are also crossovers. In the first of the series, *The Lion, the Witch and the Wardrobe* (1950), the children step – or indeed fall, there's a lot of falling into fantasy worlds! – through the back of a wardrobe from their English middle class 1940s' world into Narnia, caught in the grip of an ice age. Narnia later becomes a battleground for the fight between good and evil which is conceived of by Lewis in highly Christian terms, with the lion Aslan as the sacrificed Christ.

J.R.R. Tolkien's *The Hobbit* (1937) and *The Lord of the Rings* (1954/5) have been much blamed – unfairly in my view – for the plethora of elf-inundated fantasy that has appeared since *The Lord of the Rings* became a cult book in the 1960s. *The Hobbit* is a delightful book, a gentle and surprisingly humorous precursor to *The Lord of the Rings*, which is altogether darker. Tolkien's sonorous, unhurried prose was exploited most effectively in an extraordinarily dramatic radio adaptation of *The Lord of the Rings* in the early 1980s.

Just in these few examples taken from the classics of fantasy literature we can see the wide range of landscapes and inhabitants: fishes and caddis flies and large alarming female figures with bizarre names like Mrs Doasyouwouldbedoneby in a watery world of rocks and seaweed; anxious rabbits, philosophical caterpillars, vengeful queens and henpecked husbands all living underground in a world whose dimensions change at a terrifying rate; frozen wastes, frozen creatures, ruined castles, emerald cities, armies of the dead ...

Contemporary fantasies

Now let's look at some fantasy of the last twenty years or so. Some of these works I will be looking at in more detail during the course of the book, using them as examples of different aspects of the art and craft of writing. But because I don't think there is any hard and fast definition of what fantasy is, then it seems to me that it could be helpful to have an overview of what people consider to be contemporary fantasy. Of course if you want to write fantasy then you already have your own ideas of what fantasy consists of, but it might turn out to be a wider field than you thought.

Nowadays fantasy comes in all shapes and sizes. With the proliferation of communications media in different forms and, in particular, the explosion in computer technology of the last fifteen or so years, the picture is very different from what it was in the days of the nineteenth-century fantasists, or indeed when Tolkien was toiling over the creation of Mordor.

Many writers nowadays write series of books. This is nothing new: after all, the *Tarzan* books are a series and, while *The Lord of the Rings* cannot be described as a series, it is not a single volume but consists of three books: *The Fellowship of the Ring, The Two Towers* and *The Return of the King*. However, trilogies, or series of four or five or – heaven help us – even more, seem to be the norm rather than the exception. Let us hope that this is related to the vitality of the writing and the enthusiasm of the readers rather than to such non-fantasy elements as safe markets and no-risk publishing.

Some of the books we will be looking at later appear in series, such as Michael Moorcock's *Elric of Melniboné* (1972). Moorcock's novels and stories abound with reference, cross-reference and counter-reference, not just within but across the multitudinous series that he writes.

Tanith Lee is another wonderfully prolific writer, at ease equally with short stories, single novels and with series of novels. Her series include the five novels that she started with the sinister, haunting *Death's Master*. These novels, like much of Moorcock's work, are richly detailed and obliquely humorous. There is much wit and humour to be found in contemporary fantasy, even outside well-known 'comic' fantasy writers such as Terry Pratchett. Pratchett is another series man. Indeed his Discworld seems inexhaustible as a source of stories. And so far, with his eleventh, or is it twelfth? (it is hard to keep count), his inventiveness and his fund of jokes too seem inexhaustible.

There is magic in all the above; magic used for good, for bad, or for comic effect. There is also magic in Robert Holdstock's *Lavondyss* (1988) and in Ursula Le Guin's *Tehanu* (1990). In *Lavondyss* Holdstock explores the same piece of primaeval woodland, Ryhope Wood, and the mythagos, or myth images it contains, as he did in his previous novel, *Mythago Wood*, which won the World Fantasy Award in 1986. He has followed it with stories and another novel set in the same world. Yet these are not exactly a series. Like the relationship between, say, Le Guin's *Tehanu* and the earlier three Earthsea novels, each one is a response to the others, a further exploration of themes and images. With its female protagonist Tallis Keeton, *Lavondyss* offers a response to the male gaze of *Mythago Wood*, and is extraordinarily emotionally engaging (or devastating!). *Tehanu*, set on an outlying island of the Earthsea archipelago, queries the very basis of Earthsea's laws of magic.

But fantasy offers opportunities for those who do not plan or execute their work on the large scale of trilogies, series, or novels related to each other. Amongst readers of fantasy and science fiction there is a healthy appetite for short fiction. Fantasy and science fiction are very plastic forms: any length, it seems, can find a niche. There are lots of short stories, and collections of short stories. In the 1970s there were collections with titles like *Amazons!* (edited by Jessica Salmonson), sword and sorcery for fantasy fans whose consciousnesses had been raised by the women's movement. There are the literary anthologies, with resonant titles like *Other Edens* (three volumes in the late 1980s), edited by Christopher Evans and Robert Holdstock. Now, in our post-punk, self-mocking end-of-the-century days, there are collections with titles like *Chicks in Chainmail*, edited by Esther Friesner, with a disclaimer printed on the back cover: 'The Publisher wishes it known that the title for this volume was chosen by the editor and not by him. As a sensitive New Age Guy in good standing it would simply never occur to him to propose such a title, and he was shocked – *shocked* – that it did to others.'

Serious, sardonic, high literary or mass populist, you will find them all on the fantasy shelves. You will find whole shelves of sagas running on from one volume to another, some of which you cannot imagine anyone buying, but buy them they obviously must; you will find anthologies of shorts. You will also find, in increasing numbers now, graphic novels. Sometimes these are full-length stories, sometimes they are published in serial form. They have a wide range: from the mystical landscapes of the French artist Moebius to the urban tensions of John Wagner's and Alan Grant's Mega City One in *2000 AD* and the *Judge Dredd* volumes. On the whole the graphic novels and serial comics are the product of collaborative work between writers and artists, such as Wagner, Grant, Alan Moore, Alan Davis, Kevin O'Neill, Brendan McCarthy and others. And you will also find an ever-increasing amount of fantasy-based interactive computer games. These are different, of course, from the written (and illustrated) word, but they too have their strange and haunting landscapes, their hidden secrets, their places and people of power and magic. The actual form and shape of fantasy, it seems, is constantly changing, shifting and appearing in different guises: reflecting its subject matter, perhaps, in its magical-seeming transformations. But one thing is certain: whatever form it takes, fantasy speaks to people. It is up to you, now, to find a voice within that language.

2
Creating and building a fantasy world

Knowing your world

How do you set about creating a fantasy world? Imagine you were writing a mainstream realistic novel set in contemporary times in, say, the northwest of England. It is, perhaps, about a woman whose life has changed in all sorts of small ways as a result of getting a job in a local supermarket while her husband has become long-term unemployed; it also deals with the insights she gains into the difficulties experienced by her own mother when her father was invalided out of the army half way through the war.

Imagine. Then think of some of the things you would not need to say in the novel but that you would know in the back of your mind. And that you would expect your readers to know. You would know, for example, the outcome of the Second World War. You would know that in Britain a lot of women went out to work during the war and then were pushed back into the home and domesticity in the early 1950s. You would know that Britain is an island, that it is criss-crossed by a network of motorways and trunk roads and that if your heroine's mother lives in Birmingham then your heroine would be able to pop down and see her every so often without too much difficulty. You would know that if her children were aged twelve and fourteen then they would be at secondary school. You would know that we live on a planet that circles a sun situated towards the end of one of the outer arms of a spiral galaxy, and that the time taken for its orbit is what we call a year, and that the earth itself is orbited by a smaller planet, the moon, which waxes and wanes over the course of a month and influences, amongst other things, the movement of our seas in tides. You probably wouldn't even mention any of these things in your novel. They would be taken for granted by you and your readership.

In a fantasy novel nothing like this can be taken for granted. Your reader will know nothing about: the patterns of female employment in your created world, or educational policy, or transport infrastructure. If it is important that she knows about these things, then you must tell her. The chances are that employment, education and transport policies do not loom large in your fantasy novel; those aspects of life are more likely to be represented in your novel about a woman who lives in the northwest of England and has just got a job in a local supermarket.

But the sun which your planet orbits in your fantasy novel will certainly loom large, and your reader will need to know about it.

Your reader will need to know all the geographical, historical, cultural and linguistic details that will make your world seem real. Is this a contradiction in terms? A fantasy world that seems real? No. A fantasy writer more than any other kind of writer needs to make her readers believe in the existence of her world, for she has no shared assumptions to rely on. Her words are the bedrock of her readers' belief.

How do you convey this information? Well, what is wrong with a straightforward description? If your planet revolves round a dying sun, or if it has two moons, then say so. If your characters have travelled back through time, and find themselves trudging along the long straight Roman roads of the southwest of England, then say so. The building up of a world in words can be done in a perfectly straightforward way: there is no need to do it through dialogue, in which one character tells another something that both of them must already know ('As you know,' said the pilgrim, 'our earth circles a dying sun and so ...'). The reader is not a fool and does not need to be tricked. You must remember that the reader comes to your story, or your novel, with a willing suspension of disbelief. Your reader will believe anything you care to tell her, as long as it is not stupid or inconsistent, or told in such a way that the author implies the reader is such a fool that she won't notice fake dialogue when she reads it. If your planet circles a dying sun, then say: 'The planet circled a dying sun ...'

Most readers are tolerant creatures. They come to a book or story wanting to like it. Not so editors: I find that I become an irascible, nit-picking reader when I am reading editorially. 'As you know, I became the guardian of the magic ring when ...'

infuriates me. If the others know, then why is she telling them?

On the other hand, who wants to wade through page after page of geography or history text book, particularly if not all the details lovingly vouchsafed to your readers are going to form an integral part of your story? Who needs to know the annual rainfall, type of forests and evolutionary history of the intelligent four-footed furry inhabitants of your northern continent if the whole action of your story takes place on your southern continent?

Research is important. And it is not difficult. You will find that there are a considerable number of fantasy writers who have been students or teachers of this or that period of history. (Barbara Hambly, for example, specialised in mediaeval history for her master's degree.) It is not necessary to read heavy tomes on the past, for any good books of social history will give you ideas about dress, or food, or architecture. Military history, the history of trade routes, animal husbandry in the Middle Ages: there are books on all these subjects. Good historical fiction can help, too. The point about all this is that if, for example, you wish your characters to live in a mediaeval-type fortified city, then rather than wracking your brains to invent one fresh onto your drawing board, how much more realistic it will be if you use the plans of a real fortified city as a model for your invented one. If it really existed, then your readers will be convinced by its apparent naturalness, its detail, its appropriateness. Libraries, although they may not be open for such long hours as they used to be, are still free. The difficult bit comes when you start incorporating your research into your fiction. It is considerably more difficult than reading lots of books and taking notes on them. It requires time, instinct and lots of practice.

Ways of building your world

There is of course no absolutely correct award-winning way to create your fantasy world. I think all writers share the aim of creating a world that their readers will not only believe in but will want to lose themselves in for long periods of time, but how they create that world varies as widely as the individual writers. One way of writing a book is to know as much as you possibly can know about your characters and the setting before you embark on it. Margaret Atwood once spoke about writing in this way, describing how she would familiarise herself with a character's antecedents (childhood, parentage, even ancestors), learning the history of the character before putting her in a novel. A great deal of this information would not appear in the novel. Now this is completely different from the kind of writing, perhaps most commonly found in thrillers, in which certain information is known to the author and is deliberately withheld from the reader. The latter is all very well if the story is structured around the protagonist/reader cunningly nosing out this information, but is rather annoying when the whole plot revolves around the protagonist/reader suddenly discovering at the last minute that the murder victim, apparently alone in the world and penniless, had in fact recently come into a large fortune and had been married in secret to the woman heavily disguised as a motiveless and minor character and mentioned casually two hundred pages earlier. This, I think, is cheating, and is done by some writers who should know better. The equivalent in fantasy is, 'Whoops, I forgot to mention in volume one that the silver sword loses its magic properties if its blade is dipped in running water on the third Thursday of the month'. But I'm getting ahead of myself and leading us towards plotting.

The kind of knowledge that Margaret Atwood brings to her fictional worlds gives those worlds a kind of solidity. Her writing is at once clear and dense. You can imagine that all her characters do in fact have a past, they have a history that makes them into what they are on the page in front of you. This is as true of the characters in her future imagined state of Gilead in *The Handmaid's Tale* as it is of the characters in her mystic forest in *Surfacing*, and of the characters in her novels that are set in contemporary Toronto (*Cat's Eye*, *The Robber Bride*). Margaret Atwood is a writer devoted to a certain kind of realism. Maybe you're thinking, ah, but she doesn't write fantasy, but what I want to stress here is that fantasy writing needs realism. Fantasy writing needs characters with histories, it needs mountains with geological strata within them, it needs ways of speaking that are rooted in cultures developed over hundreds, or thousands of years. A fantasy world, even more than a fictional world that reflects or represents our own world, needs solidity. If you set your story in our own world you don't need to work terribly hard to get your readers to believe in it; after all, they live in it. But they need to be utterly convinced by your fantasy world. You, the writer, must know it inside out, its crevices and abysses and dark hidden places.

Margaret Atwood's is one way of writing. You could say that at the other end of the scale in terms of method is Ursula K. Le Guin. Listen to her response when asked by the editor of a magazine to describe for his readers how she planned the Earthsea world, how she developed the languages, and whether she kept lists of places and characters and so on.

> To which I returned some kind of garble-garble, of which I recall only one sentence,
> 'But I didn't plan anything, I found it.'
> Editor (not unnaturally): 'Where?'
> Me: 'In my subconscious.'

She goes on to describe this finding. In 1964 she wrote a story about a wizard which was set on an island, but didn't pay much attention to the setting as it was not relevant. Soon after that she wrote another story, and of this one she says:

> ... I had fun playing around a bit with the scenery, and with the old island ladies drinking rushwash tea, and so on. It was set on an island called Sattins, which I knew to be one of an outlying group east of the main archipelago. The main character, a dragon known first as Mr Underhill and then, when his nature is revealed, by his true name Yevaud, came from a westerly isle called Pendor. I did not much bother with all the islands that I knew lay between Sattins and Pendor, and north and south of them. They weren't involved ... ('Dreams Must Explain Themselves', *The Language of the Night*, p.40)

It seems almost incredible that such a complex archipelago (complex not just geographically but historically, culturally and any which way you care to think) should have grown round, or, as Ursula Le Guin puts it, should have been discovered round the tiny island of Sattins with its little old ladies drinking their rushwash tea.

In a way you can hardly imagine two approaches to writing more at variance with each other than that of Margaret Atwood and Ursula Le Guin. Yet both of them create worlds – the archipelagoes of Earthsea, the future north America of Gilead, and present-day Canada. It is important to remember that this last is also a created world; for language creates, it cannot simply represent. In other words there is no such thing as a simple representation. These worlds are solid and imaginatively true even although they may not exist in the 'real' world.

I have chosen these two writers deliberately for their difference of approach, because I want to stress that there is no single correct way to write, no sure-fire means of getting down on to paper the inner truth of your imagined world. You want your imagined world to appear natural, to appear as if it could not be any other way. The names in your world, the language, the things that the language describes, must be all of a piece, they must seem to have grown together organically. Here is an example of that organic interweaving, as Ursula Le Guin talks about the tea they drink in Earthsea:

> There are words, like rushwash tea, for which I can offer no explanation. They simply drink rushwash tea there; that's what it's called, like lapsang soochong or Lipton's here. Rushwash is a Hardic word, of course. If you press me, I will explain that it comes from the rushwash bush, which grows both wild and cultivated everywhere south of Enlad, and bears a small round leaf which when dried and steeped yields a pleasant brownish tea. I did not know this before I wrote the foregoing sentence. Or did I know it, and simply never thought about it? What's in a name? A lot, that's what. (*The Language of the Night* p.42)

In the novels we are not told that the rushwash leaf yields a pleasant brownish tea, etc. etc., but we are not at all surprised to discover it now, when Le Guin explains her working methods. It seems perfectly natural, and the drinking of it is as natural as our drinking Lipton's. Both the action, and the name, appear natural, unforced. This is part of Le Guin's skill: we don't have to wrench our minds and contort our souls into believing in these goings-on in Earthsea. It is easy to believe in little old ladies sitting around drinking rushwash tea. And it is all consistent, because of course – I love that 'of course' – rushwash comes from the Hardic, as you would expect. And Hardic is a language that doesn't have its hearers' ears tied up in knots. Ursula Le Guin is suggesting that language must be simple, suitable and consistent, and that the names of characters and things within the world where that language is spoken must also be simple, suitable and consistent. For why? Partly at least because names are very important. And anyone who has read the Earthsea books will know that in Earthsea names are very important indeed.

It is a mistake to imagine that another world needs out-landish trappings. What we want is a world in which we can imagine we are living. Personally, I would be one of the ones sipping rushwash tea, but I'm sure there are plenty of others who would want to be casting spells, chatting with dragons, seeking the Grail or whatever most takes their fancy. Those are the kinds of readers you want, those are the kinds of readers you must create. A writer creates her own readers as she writes; or in other words, you get the readers you deserve.

Names, speech, language

There are as many ways to create a fantasy world as there are fantasy worlds in existence, and you must find the way that best suits you. I'm going to end this chapter with a few examples of how some writers introduce their worlds to their readers. But first I'm going to offer some don'ts, some on no account do this or that, some examples of pitfalls and tripwires that lurk in the path of the unwary writer. And then, of course, you must feel free to disregard these warnings if you so wish.

For this I'm going to draw on the work of David Langford who, I think, has probably read more contemporary fantasy, heroic and otherwise, than any other critic extant, and surely deserves the title of Heroic Reader.

Let's start with names. Anything that looks unpronounce-able should be avoided; go for simplicity. Ged, to stick with Ursula Le Guin, or Bilbo, or Frodo or Gandalf. David Langford warns against the 'improbably placed' apostrophe, blaming the major influence of 'A'nne M'cCaffrey'. He quotes from *Moreta*:

> '...Orlith says you've done a good job, A'dan .... You were marvellous assistants, M'barak, D'Itan, B'greal!' ... ('The Dragonhiker's Guide to Battlefield Covenant at Dune's Edge: Odyssey Two', in *Let's Hear It for the Deaf Man*, p.23)

Apostrophes or no, these names sound simply silly. You can't imagine that they're real names and, as our Heroic Reader points out, they are dished out to a host of minor characters, walk-on parts, who don't need names anyway.

It is difficult to make up names. It is difficult even to make them up for characters who inhabit a recognisable contemporary world, and considerably more so for characters in a fantasy world. There's the not-exactly-subtle Lord Foul, the evil lord (surprise surprise) in Stephen Donaldson's Thomas Covenant books (and of course Covenant has to be a hero in order to fulfil the promise of his name). Post- *Pilgrim's Progress* I think a reader would be justified in feeling insulted by such blatant ascription of goodness and badness. In an article called 'Untrue Names' David Langford takes exception to Guy Gavriel Kay's Aileron ('Kay says he's a High King but I know he's just an aeroplane's wing-flap') , but even such a linguist as Tolkien has a character called Thingol (*Let's Hear It for the Deaf Man*, p.28); names are not easy to invent and you have to steer between silliness on one side and portentousness on the other. Indeed Kay's Aileron really can't win: not only is he saddled with the -on ending (a science fictional favourite which is a side effect of particle physics, Langford suggests), but also the Ail- prefix. Ail-, Al- and El- are to be regularly found in SF and fantasy (Tolkien's Elrond is another example, and Moorcock's Elric), echoing perhaps that great fantasy original of H.P. Lovecraft's, the mad Arab Abdul Al-Hazrad, author of the legendary *Necronomicon*. These prefixes do indeed have resonances with Arab names, and thus provide a touch of Eastern 'exoticism', one that is perhaps not entirely spurious when you consider the influence of *The Thousand and One Nights* on Western literature in general and on fantasy in particular.

When you are giving your characters words to speak – and what is the use of a book without pictures or conversations? as Alice famously wondered – a similar careful navigation has to be undertaken between the dangers of overweirdness and the dangers of humdrumness. (As for pictures, on no account include your line drawings of fairies and mermaids when you submit the manuscript of your novel.) It is amazing what contortions of grammar some writers force their characters through to give an impression of – what? antiquity? mediaevalness? fantasy? But then as offputting as the stilted, or incorrect, archaisms, is a language that sounds as if it is being spoken by Mr and Mrs Normal of Milton Keynes at the end of the twentieth century (unless that's where they've come from and you're writing a crossover story). Language is as revealing of thought, culture, way of life, as it is itself moulded by them. People who live in another world do not speak in the same way as people who live in this world; the trick, then, is to provide them with speech that does not flow from a life lived in the 1990s, but one that sounds easy and natural in the mouths of the people who live in your created world. Try this:

> 'So then after a while Ogion came back to Re Albi. And when he told me the story, he said to me, "Ever since that day, I have wondered if anyone, man or dragon, has been farther west than west; and who we are, and where our wholeness lies ." ... Are you getting hungry, Therru? There's a good sitting place, it looks like, up there where the road turns. Maybe from there we'll be able to see Gont Port, away down at the foot of the mountain. It's a big city, even bigger than Valmouth. We'll sit down when we get to the turn, and rest a bit.'

This is the woman Tenar speaking to the child Therru in Ursula Le Guin's *Tehanu*: the language is natural-sounding and most importantly perhaps it has the rhythm of spoken language. You can actually imagine someone saying these words. And there is some heightened language as well: the words of Ogion, who is a wizard, have a different rhythm from Tenar's words: 'farther west than west ...', and then the two rhetorical (but important to the story) questions. Ogion's speech is more poetical than Tenar's, it hints at magic and mystery, but it's not difficult, either to hear as spoken words or to understand. Note the names as well: Ogion, Re Albi, Therru, Gont, Valmouth. We are in a world that is not our own world, but we are not made to feel strangers by being confronted with people and places whose names we can't even pronounce.

In his novels *Mythago Wood* and *Lavondyss* Robert Holdstock has created a world in which what we perceive as the normal laws of time no longer operate. It is an ancient world which owes much to myth and legend. An appropriate language was needed. In this interview, conducted by Lisa Tuttle, he talks about struggling to invent such a language:

> I was trying to invent a really old-sounding language, resonant words which would reflect something very primeval, primordial, from the time of shamanism, about 10,000 BC ... I looked at Welsh, I thought about Gaelic, and I tried to make some educated guesses about earlier forms, and then I allowed a fusion with the unconscious. Words would come into my head while I was having a bath or walking up the street – or sleeping!

– and these words seemed to have their own structure and
form. They sound right – and other people have told me they
sound right to them, too. So, although it is a completely
invented language, it would be wonderful to think I might be
tapping a racial memory of the first language! (*City Limits*,
October 1988)

It is not just the kind of language, the vocabulary and speech
patterns that you give to your characters that is crucial. It is just
as important to get right the third person, authorial voice, the
narrative voice that your reader must feel comfortable with.

Here is a description, from Michael Moorcock's *Elric of
Melniboné*, of The Ship Which Sails Over Land and Sea, a
magical ship which fulfils most wonderfully the promise of its
name:

> The ship was tall and slender and she was delicate. Her rails,
> masts and bulwarks were exquisitely carved and obviously not
> the work of a mortal craftsman. Though built of wood, the
> wood was not painted but naturally shone blue and black and
> green and a kind of deep smoky red; and her rigging was the
> colour of seaweed and there were veins in the planks of her
> polished deck, like the roots of trees, and the sails on her three
> tapering masts were as fat and white and light as clouds on a
> fine summer day. (p.111)

This is unhurried, unanxious prose. It tells us quite a lot about
the ship: it conjures up physical specifics (rails, masts, bul-
warks, rigging, planks, sails) and also suggests the ship's
supernatural provenance. The rigging that is the colour of seaweed and the veins in the planks like the roots of trees remind
the reader of what we have been told: that the ship was built
by the elementals of Water and of Earth. There is no fancy
vocabulary, and the description ends with a simile that is
unpretentious, unremarkable even, but that adds the idea of
airiness, of flight, to the description: 'sails ... as fat and white
and light as clouds on a fine summer day.

There is no eldritch or argute here, no mystification.
Instead, simple words like tall, blue, fat; and Moorcock even
gets away with 'a kind of deep smoky red', which coming
from a writer of less assurance than Moorcock might seem
vague. Here, I think you are able to know exactly what is
meant. This is a writer, it seems to me, who takes pleasure in
what he is describing.

It often helps to read your book, or story, out loud, particularly passages of direct speech. Or indeed to tape it and play it back to yourself as you're working on it. The novelist and short story writer Michael Carson recommends this method. If you can't say the words you have given your characters to say without sounding like a three-tongued single-nostrilled water vole, then start again. Unless of course your characters happen to be three-tongued, single-nostrilled water voles, in which case you are a skilled writer, but will probably never be a best-selling one.

To sum up: keep your language natural and simple. And if you get the language right, everything will follow from that.

A word of advice on maps

The only other major pitfall to avoid at this stage is spending all your time embellishing the map you plan as your frontispiece, adding a swamp here, a dark forest there and drawing in the contour lines on the mountains. Start with a basic map if you need one, but don't let your map work distract you from getting on with your story.

Some beginnings

How do you introduce your readers to a world that may be incredibly familiar to you, after all, you've been living in it for years, but which is completely strange to them? Let's look at a few beginnings.

I can't resist following Ursula Le Guin's example, and so will start by quoting the opening sentences of *The Hobbit*:

> In a hole in the ground there lived a hobbit. Not a nasty, dirty, wet hole, filled with the ends of worms and an oozy smell, nor yet a dry, bare, sandy hole with nothing in it to sit down on or to eat: it was a hobbit-hole, and that means comfort.

As Le Guin has so beautifully put it, this allows us to arrive, by however peculiar a fashion, at the truth, through a story that promises in its opening sentences humour and generosity as well as magic.

And now the openings of some of the novels and short stories I shall be referring you to later on in this book:

The changeling's decision to steal a dragon and escape was born, though she did not know it then, the night the children met to plot the death of their supervisor.

She had lived in the steam dragon plant for as long as she could remember. Each dawn she was marched with the other indentured minors from their dormitory in Building 5 to the cafeteria for a breakfast she barely had time to choke down before work. Usually she was then sent to the cylinder machine shop for polishing labor, but other times she was assigned to Building 12, where the black iron bodies were inspected and oiled before being sent to the erection shop for final assembly. The abdominal tunnels were too small for an adult. It was her duty to crawl within them to swab out and then grease those dark passages. She worked until sunset and sometimes later if there was a particularly important dragon under contract.

Her name was Jane. (*The Iron Dragon's Daughter*, Michael Swanwick, 1993)

I remember how, that night, I lay awake in the wagon-lit in a tender, delicious ecstasy of excitement, my burning cheek pressed against the impeccable linen of the pillow and the pounding of my heart mimicking that of the great pistons cease-lessly thrusting the train that bore me through the night, away from Paris, away from girlhood, away from the white, enclosed quietude of my mother's apartment, into the unguessable country of marriage. ('The Bloody Chamber' in *The Bloody Chamber and other adult tales*, Angela Carter, 1979)

In both these openings the reader is placed at once at the heart of a machine age, not perhaps what you might expect from fantasy. Both have a nineteenth-century feel to them, conjuring up pictures we are already familiar with from books, films, pictures, of child labour in the cotton mills of Lancashire in Michael Swanwick's novel, and, in Angela Carter's story, of wealthy Europeans crisscrossing the Continent in luxurious trains in the days before mass tourism.

While Angela Carter speaks as a fabulist, with an ironic and playful awareness of the reader's knowledge of the story of Bluebeard and his wives, Swanwick gives us the grim details of Jane's life in the factory. If it wasn't for the word 'changeling', you would hardly know this was fantasy at all. Yet what is striking, what is most important, is the way the reader is poised on the very brink of an abyss right at the beginning: murder in the one; unguessable, possibly indescribable, sexual knowledge in the other. Fantasy allows this, opening up for the reader, right at the beginning, as we see in these two examples, a road that leads direct into the heart of things.

> Sky and land had the same sallow bluish tinge, soaked in cold light from a vague white sun. It was late summer, but summer might never have come here. The few trees were bare of leaves and birds. The cindery grassless hills rolled up and down monotonously. Their peaks gleamed dully, their dips were full of mist. It was a land for sad songs and dismal rememberings, and, when the night came, for nightmares and hallucinations.
> ('Northern Chess', 1979, in *Women as Demons*, Tanith Lee, 1989)

This is a more traditional fantasy landscape, empty, wasted, haunted, and probably cursed. This is a landscape that speaks of bad magic. The reader waits: who will ride into this landscape, and how will it be restored?

> Cal Cara Kerig was five years old when she saw her mother killed. Her mother was mad, Cara was told, and madness was a disruption of the universe.
> It was in the last days of the Gara han Gara, whose name meant Even Pressure over the Land. There was a long drought: rain did not fall for over half a year and the rice growing in steps up the canyon walls began to die. Cara's mother went to the wells of vision, which were forbidden to women, to find why the drought had come. (*The Warrior Who Carried Life*, Geoff Ryman, 1985)

There might be bad magic here: we do not yet know why the drought had come. But there is certainly cruelty, murder, deception, and a politics that denies women a part. Cara is lied to: her mother was killed because she went to a place forbidden to women. Again, the reader seems to be poised on the brink of an abyss: how will Cara live, having seen her own mother killed? How will she survive the knowledge of why the drought had come?

> It is the colour of a bleached skull, his flesh; and the long hair which flows below his shoulders is milk-white. From the tapering, beautiful head stare two slanting eyes, crimson and moody, and from the loose sleeves of his yellow gown emerge two slender hands, also the colour of bone, resting on each arm of a

seat which has been carved from a single, massive ruby.
(Michael Moorcock, *Elric of Melniboné*, 1972)

The mood is one of decadence and opulence. Death is there in the first image.

Gil knew that it was only a dream. There was no reason for her to feel fear – she knew that the danger, the chaos, the blind, sickening nightmare terror that filled the screaming night were not real; this city with its dark, unfamiliar architecture, these fleeing crowds of panic-stricken men and women who shoved her aside, unseeing, were only the vivid dregs of an overloaded subconscious, wraiths that would melt with daylight.

She knew all this; nevertheless, she was afraid. (*The Time of the Dark*, Barbara Hambly, 1982)

The second paragraph comes in the nick of time. Gil's fear, even when she has rationalised away her vision of the first paragraph, signals to the reader that this is very probably not a dream. The rational explanation, based on Gil's apparently certain knowledge, must be wrong. Her fear is too strong. So what is all this, wonders the reader – and reads on.

After Farmer Flint of the Middle Valley died, his widow stayed on at the farmhouse. Her son had gone to sea and her daughter had married a merchant of Valmouth, so she lived alone at Oak Farm. People said she had been some kind of great person in the foreign land she came from, and indeed the mage Ogion used to stop by Oak Farm to see her; but that didn't count for much, since Ogion visited all sorts of nobodies. (*Tehanu*, Ursula K. Le Guin, 1990)

An extraordinary amount of information is packed into this first paragraph, not only about the circumstances of the woman who is as yet unnamed, but about the kind of society she now lives in. The reader learns not just that it is a society of farmers, merchants and sailors, but that it is a society that, like any other, is shot through with particular prejudices and snobberies. One area in which these are expressed is people's interest in the behaviour of their mages. Ordinary enough, you might think, yet this detail of social observation is the seed from which grows the novel's central concern with the use and abuse of magical powers, and its exploration of the meaning of magic and its relation to power.

Questions of evil, cruelty, sexuality and mortality, run through *Tehanu* as indeed they do through some of the other works just quoted from, most obviously Geoff Ryman's *The Warrior Who Carried Life* and also Michael Swanwick's *The Iron Dragon's Daughter*. But how different are their styles, and how different their openings!

And finally, from the opening sequence of Robert Holdstock's *Lavondyss*:

> The bright moon, hanging low over Barrow Hill, illuminated the snow-shrouded fields and made the winter land seem to glow with faint light. It was a lifeless, featureless place, and yet the shapes of the fields were clear, marked out by the moon-shadow of the dark oak hedges that bordered them. Distantly, from that shadow round the meadow called The Stumps, the ghostly figure began to move again, following a hidden track over the rise of ground, then moving left, into tree cover. It stood there, just visible now to the old man who watched it from Stretley Farm; watching back. The cloak it wore was dark, the hood pulled low over its face. As it moved for the second time, coming closer to the farmhouse, it left the black wood behind. It was stooped, against the Christmas cold, perhaps. Where it walked it left a deep furrow in the fresh snow.

There are figures in this landscape, real figures however ghostly they may seem, for the hooded figure not only watches but is watched by the old man. But it is the land and what it contains that are presented to the reader as central, as imbued with mystery and with magic and with secrets waiting to be revealed.

What can be learned from these eight examples of fantasy novels and stories published in the last twenty-five years? You can hardly compare one with another, for where one writer packs information into the opening sentences, another imbues them with atmosphere; where one concentrates on character, another gives us landscape; where one shows intellectual conflict, another gives us intensity of emotion. But in all of them, I think, there is a sense of words chosen so carefully that the resulting mix of images, ideas and rhythms in the very language suggest that if you read on you will enter a world that is well worth exploring. In each of them the writer's fantasy world is there, perhaps only hinted at but there as a presence nonetheless, in those first few words. And that is what gives those worlds their reality. Their writers believe in them.

3
Archetypes, attitudes and assumptions

Archetypes

An archetype is an original pattern from which copies are made. Fantasy writing is full of archetypes. Which is not surprising, when you consider how often fantasy tells a story of origins. And even when it is not telling a story of origins, when it is not relating an Adam and Eve in a new world story, it is set in a world that has been newly created by you, the writer. So it is not surprising that archetypes will make their appearance, because they will come, whether unbidden or deliberately sought after, from the recesses of your unconscious.

Archetypes, because they are something original, are necessarily something old, and fundamental to storytelling. What are some examples of archetypes? Questing heroes and heroines, wise old women whose advice should not be ignored, dragons flashing in over the western isles, wily young lads and lasses (who may be disguised as animals), absent mothers, wicked stepmothers, weak-willed fathers, ambitious uncles. Unicorns and sphinxes, flying horses and speaking toads. Green men: not little green men from Mars, but powerful green men, and green women, who lurk in the wildwood and are not necessarily friendly or safe.

Many of these figures will be familiar to you from fairytales, folktales and ballads, and from myth and legend. This is where modern fantasy has its roots. And although those figures may appear slightly different with each retelling – and shape-shifting after all is a central image in fantasy – their modern versions will nonetheless be nourished by the older original forms.

If you wish to explore theories of archetypes then there are plenty of sources you can go to. Carl Jung, of course, was in many ways the architect of the way that we now think about archetypes, and it was he who rooted them in the idea of the collective unconscious. Freud too was a theoretician of archetypes, although he did not call them that. And it was Freud who articulated our oedipal dreams and stripped our infantile desires of their innocence. Psychoanalysis perhaps – and not just Freud but practitioners who focussed on mothers rather than fathers, such as Karen Horney – could be said to tell us folktales of the modern age. Think of the case histories of the Wolf Man, or Dora, with their strangely universal feel, their plots that are simultaneously modern and antique.

You could read Joseph Campbell on myth and religion, or Marina Warner who, in *From the Beast to the Blonde; On Fairytales and their Tellers*, traces the history of our best-known folk and fairytales and shows how, originally, they reflected the everyday conditions of people's lives. She also shows how similar stories occur and recur in different cultures and traditions. The figures in *Cinderella*, for example – the once-favoured child cast down, the wicked stepmother, the jealous older sisters, the rejecting father – can be viewed as universal archetypes, for versions of this story appear in cultures east and west, north and south.

But you don't need to read up on the theory. Why should you? For archetypal figures are part of our own lives, if we have the eyes to see them. The family drama of early childhood is experienced by every single one of us, whatever the different circumstances of our individual lives, for everyone is born dependent and needy and everyone must experience loss and separation. This is the story of our growing up. Our relationships with the mothers and fathers, the sisters and brothers of our own lives nourish the archetypal figures that appear in fantasy as elf queens and dragon masters, centaurs and mermen, ravening wolves and talking trickster cats.

These are figures that resonate in the human mind. And one of the reasons that they are so powerful is that they are instantly recognisable.

These are figures from tales that we are familiar with, that strike chords with our own deepest childhood memories. And nowadays, in the twentieth century, these figures appear in images all around us, for many of these archetypes have been redrawn for film and television. Walt Disney has been enormously influential in our current imaging of them. Think of the cartoon portrayal of the wicked stepmother in *Snow White*, for example. Stories that in previous centuries were read or told are now disseminated through images on television and film, in soap operas, cartoons, advertisements. This is now our oral tradition, and one that writers ignore at their peril.

Modern fairytales

In the next chapter I will be looking at the plots of stories and showing how old and trusted plots can be used for modern and surprising tales. In the same way, original archetypal figures, the characters we meet in fairytale and folktale, can also be reworked for our own age. A fabulist like Angela Carter, in her collection *The Bloody Chamber and other adult tales*, draws out of the fairytales she retells the dark threads of violence, corruption, cruelty and sexual passion that are often hidden in the anodyne versions told to children. In these tales the present day is ornately intertwined with the misty history out of which the folktales first came. It is not easy to mix the new with the old, and we have seen some of the dangers and pitfalls in the previous chapter. Angela Carter's bold, baroque writing style is ideally suited to this form of storytelling which is at once transhistorical and yet rooted in the materiality of people's lives. She throws together castles, telephones, agents in New York and blood-ridden underground chambers, and, in the title story, gives us a marvellous model of a pioneering mother who gallops to her daughter's rescue as the waves wash over the causeway.

Fairytales lend to fantasy writers not just the power of the archetypal figures within them, but also a structure that is very common in fantasy: that of movement in the story from separateness and fragmentation and loss, to healing and wholeness.

There is a wonderful recent anthology edited by Terri Windling (responsible for the earlier, award-winning *Elsewhere* volumes of fantasy stories) which includes stories and poems from writers known within and outside the fantasy genre, such as: Louise Gluck, Jane Gardam, Emma Bull, Tappan King, Tanith Lee, Patricia A McKillip, Kristine Kathryn Rusch, Midori Snyder, Jane Yolen and Terri Windling herself. *The Armless Maiden and Other Tales for Childhood's Survivors* is an anthology about childhood that is most definitely not for children. Through retelling tales such as *Donkeyskin, Hansel and Gretel, Snow White* and the title story (*The Armless Maiden* is an African version of the European *The*

Handless Maiden and *The Girl with Silver Hands*) the writers uncover the grim terrain of abused childhood and chart the rough, rugged and lonely tracks that lead out of it. Terri Windling says of it that the anthology grew 'out of conversations and correspondence, out of shared tales, artwork, memories and dreams.' It was like creating a collage, she says, with her own voice as background for 'the stories that have meant the most to me in twenty years of working with fairy tales. Arranged against that background are the answering voices of thirty-three other writers.' The retold fairytales and folktales in this collection tell us stories of survival and of achievement. They explore the pain of children cruelly exploited, but they also recount the stories of their growing up and the piecing together of their shattered selves into women and men capable of loving and being loved.

Nonetheless, rich though fairy and folktales are, not everyone wants to be retelling them and the chances are that even if you do wish to include archetypal figures in your writing you may well want to include other figures, too.

Landscape

Archetypal landscapes, like the archetypal figures just discussed, appear in all our ancient stories and serve as the models for landscapes in modern fantasies. In a great deal of fantasy the landscape of the story plays as important a role as the characters in the story. It is almost as if the landscape itself is a character.

Sometimes the landscape embodies qualities that play their part in the story. In an article on Alan Garner's *The Weirdstone of Brisingamen*, the writer David Profumo, remarking on the brooding presence of Alderley Edge in all Garner's work, imbuing it, he suggests, with a 'hard topographic strength', goes on to say that in *The Weirdstone* 'the ancient properties of the land are seen as decent and true ...' (*The Sunday Times*, 23 July 1995).

The primaeval woodland of Robert Holdstock's *Mythago Wood* and *Lavondyss* provides a power drawn from prehistory that together with human emotions creates the physical manifestation of an archetype from the collective unconscious, or mythago, as it is called in these novels.

These two writers have found their inspiration in real, ancient landscapes. Both of them recognise the power of the archetypal nature of these landscapes and have made that a central part of their stories. Far from being 'an escape back to nature', this can be a way of investigating, through fantasy, the dialectic between present and past, not just in an individual, but in a community or indeed in a landscape. A writer like Robert Holdstock, in the novels mentioned above, takes a patch of old woodland and draws the reader deep into the heart of it, alongside his characters in the present day, deeper and deeper back into time so that the woodland itself becomes the central organising symbol in the work. Landscape does not have to be relegated to decoration: landscape can hold and divulge meanings for the characters in a story, whether it is the ancient woodland of the British Isles, or the wide open spaces of the American mid-west. As so many writers and film makers know (and not just writers of fantasy) people have a complex and often passionate relationship with the land and nature, and that relationship can be the subject of a story, not just the background for it.

It comes as no surprise that both Alan Garner and Robert Holdstock trace their involvement with the landscape back to childhood. Garner was severely ill for much of his childhood and, as David Profumo said, 'As he lay on his sickbed, sometimes close to death, the young Garner contemplated those ancient rockfaces of the Pennine shelf and experienced what sounds like a geological epiphany: "on that hill, the universe opened".'

And Robert Holdstock, who uses the area around Tenterden in rural Kent for the setting of his novels, says: 'That is my childhood landscape; that was where I had my greatest sense of freedom, and it was very formative. You know they say that when you go back you find things are smaller? That land is bigger.' (Interview with Robert Holdstock by Lisa Tuttle, *City Limits*, October, 1988) That indeed is one of the most important characteristics of his primaeval woodland: the way that it expands to become a whole, other, different world.

Fantasies are often set in depopulated landscapes whose few inhabitants are caught in a social structure that always reminds me of that period that I seemed to do over and over again in school: the feudal period with barons and castles and keeps and woolly-horned cattle and horses decked out in colourful gear. Fantasy has often been accused of being escapist, of allowing the reader (and writer) to turn from the complexities of modern life to an idealised time when there were fewer people, no traffic and everything was much simpler. To a certain extent that is probably true, and some fantasies do seem very nostalgic for an idealised, dirt-, disease- and pain-free past.

Yet you will find that the depopulated landscapes of fantasy are often not escapist at all, but, if not actively imbued with qualities and characteristics, can offer a stark emptiness which points up the profound human dramas played out in them.

Wastelands of snow and ice are a recurring image in fantasy and science fiction: think of Victor Frankenstein and his rejected, vengeful monster chasing each other across the vast and irregular plains of ice in Mary Shelley's *Frankenstein*; or think of the earth envoy Genly Ai and the hermaphroditic Gethenian Estraven in Ursula Le Guin's *The Left Hand of Darkness*. They face profound questions of love, betrayal and identity as they huddle in the whiteout of a blizzard in their struggle across the snowy northern wastes of Gethen. Contemporary fantasy and science fiction writers such as Mary Gentle and Nicola Griffith, and Doris Lessing in her Canopean series, have all used powerful images of frozen landscapes as desolate backgrounds for the playing out of profound human dramas.

Can an urban landscape resonate as profoundly, or are urban landscapes both too modern and too cluttered? I think the twentieth century has seen the birth of a new archetype in the modern monster city, which has entered our dreams and nightmares, mainly through film images. From Fritz Lang's *Metropolis* through the *film noir* thrillers of the 1940s to the massive twenty-second century metropolis Mega City One of the *Judge Dredd* Comics (recently transformed, in an interesting development, into film), these are cities in which the human soul can be plumbed to its depth. Yet in written literature the neon-lit highways and beside them the dark alleyways have on the whole found their place in thriller writing, and not in fantasy.

Of course there *are* cities in fantasy stories. I was thinking about the Discworld's Ankh-Morpork, and wondering whether that has an archetypal resonance. (It certainly has an archetypal smell.) Then I thought that part of that city's archetypal power comes from the river that bisects it, that divides proud Ankh from pestilent Morpork, a river that 'even an agnostic could walk across.' The river Ankh is related to many of the great rivers of literature, as is helpfully explained in the *The Discworld Companion*: 'There are said to be some mystic rivers, one drop of which can steal a man's life away. After its turbid passage through the twin cities, the Ankh could be one of them.'

The river has an extraordinarily powerful presence in fantasy. All rivers, whether they wind down to tower'd Camelot, or run through caverns measureless to man, have an affinity with the final river, the River Styx. Rivers carry away the dead, as well as bringing life. As with the archetypal figures that we recognise both in literature and in life, so too with landscapes and with the rivers that run through them. Think of how London draws much of its mythological power from the River Thames, think of the Nile, the Rhine, the Ganges, and how they all feed the lives, the cities and the lands of the peoples who live beside them; and, of course, they feed their literatures, too.

Archetypes come from people's lives and find expression in their literatures.

It would be a mistake to think that you must find some archetypes for your story when you start out to write fantasy. This brief look at how some writers use archetypal images and figures is designed to show how ubiquitous they are, and to encourage you, the writer, to open your mind to the resonances that archetypes offer. You have only to look into your own life to find archetypal patterns. If you can, allow them to enrich your writing.

Attitudes and assumptions

In the next chapter, when I will be talking about plots and stories, I will be talking again about archetypes and how if they are to appear in a story they must have life breathed into them. Now, however, I want to move from the past into the present and consider what attitudes and assumptions you might bring to your story. In other words, how your consciousness – which itself is in constant dialogue with the culture that surrounds it – shapes your material.

Fantasy may be set in an ancient-seeming otherworld. The landscape may consist of dark forests, swift-flowing rivers and mountains that have brooded over all since the dawn of time. This land may be inhabited by dragons and wolves, by broken kings and wicked courtiers, by wizards corrupted and young men incorruptible. But you and your readers live in the contemporary world. They will be bringing attitudes and assumptions from there to what they read and you will be bringing them to what you write.

Good fantasy speaks to us now. It does not speak to us in contemporary forms of speech. I have already pointed out the pitfalls of contemporary speech forms. But it speaks to our experience and knowledge. It can perhaps speak more directly than other forms of fiction.

If, in your created world, the female characters are all languishing princesses who, after being rescued from ravening monsters, marry princes and settle into happy motherhood, it is unlikely you would keep your readers' interest for long. Stereotypes don't sustain a story. They don't say anything about our experience of the world.

Fantasy is full of stock characters, such as the dragons, wolves, kings, courtiers mentioned above. It is what you do with them that is important. Your attitude as a writer towards your material cannot be acquiescent, for if your material is to speak to contemporary readers, you must ask of it: how can this illuminate the complexities, or the vagaries of the human soul? How does this speak to me (and so to my readers)?

A couple of examples from recently published novels may make the point better than I can. First, elves: notoriously mercurial, aloof from (and condescending towards) humankind, they may offer assistance if asked but are not to be relied upon. In Michael Swanwick's *The Iron Dragon's Daughter* the elves are decadent traders in other people's bodies and souls. Their assistance comes with a price to pay, their aloofness is transformed into atrophy of the emotions, and their mercurial nature is most apparent through an eroticisation of all social intercourse. They don't just swing both ways, they swing every which way. They are players of games, and dealers of death.

I am not going to make an analogy between the elves and any particular group of people in our own world, for this is not allegory, but fiction, and the elves are ... elves. But, with their fetishisation of style and their commodification of the human body, they have an extraordinarily powerful end-of-the-century feel to them.

Second, magic. Magic is what makes the world go round, isn't it? There is good magic and bad magic, and many a trilogy charts the ongoing struggle between the two. In

Ursula Le Guin's *Tehanu*, the holding and the relinquishing, of magic powers are presented to the reader as a drama of ways of knowing, and therefore ways of inhabiting, the world. More specifically, the magic (or the refusal of it) illuminates what it means to be a woman, and what it means to be a man, in a world that has embraced masculine values at the expense of all else.

These two novels deal with the complexity of the world we live in. Representations of exploitation, corruption, cruelty and violence (and in particular violence towards children) run through both of them. One is the story of a young girl growing up, the other of a woman growing old.

This is what elves and magic can do. Do not assume anything less.

And finally, a favourite story of mine, Tanith Lee's 'Northern Chess', shakes the stereotypes out of their musty old clothes and with humour and neatness questions the attitudes and assumptions that manacle the mind, in fantasy or outside it. This story is sword and sorcery with all the trimmings, including corpses that glow in the dark with 'the witch-light of dead flesh'. But the heroine, Jaisel, does not and cannot accept 'that destiny was unchangeable'. As the rules of chess can be changed, so too can the rules of sword and sorcery, and so too can the rules of life. This story speaks to an audience that does not believe in a deterministic world; and by allowing Jaisel to fulfil the prophecy of the evil wizard Maudras, that the castle will never 'to the world's ending ... be taken by any *man*', it questions both language and attitude.

But Jaisel does not win simply because she is a woman. She has to survive in order to be able to exploit the linguistic loophole. And she survives because she thinks. She uses her intelligence, which she seems able to do (being our heroine) in the dark while being attacked from all directions: 'Some power which could make her out when she was nearly blind, but which seemed to attack randomly, inaccurately. She cast herself flat again and crawled on her belly to the head of a stair. Here, descending, she became the perfect target. No matter. Her second swordsmaster had been something of an acrobat –' (*Women as Demons*, p.269)

She is condescended to because of her sex, but she survives triumphant, whereas the knights, who have failed to think as swiftly as Jaisel, are now, alas for them, providing the witch-light by which Jaisel reads Maudras' messages. She doesn't win because she is a woman, but because women are human and therefore as capable of intelligent thought as men are.

This may seem obvious, but it is worth pointing out the dangers in not interrogating your own attitudes and assumptions. Fantasy is full of apparently familiar characters, landscapes and scenes, but because they seem familiar does not mean that they cannot be without surprises. The old forms have survived precisely because they contain deep significances, and are able to offer fresh meanings with each retelling.

On re-reading 'Northern Chess' it struck me that there is another level to it. You can see it as a story of a woman running away from her own femininity and eventually finding a way to reclaim it, triumphantly. For '...when she saw the women at their looms or in their greasy kitchens, or tangled with babies, or broken with field work, or leering out of painted masks from shadowy town doorways, Jaisel's urge to travel, to ride, to fly, to run away, increased.' (*Women as Demons*, p.258) Well, wouldn't yours? And is this story not about women and men and how they inhabit the world together?

4
Cunning plots and old stories

There are many untold stories waiting to be told. In *Wide Sargasso Sea* Jean Rhys told the story of Bertha Mason, Mr Rochester's mad hidden wife in Charlotte Bronte's *Jane Eyre*; Michèle Roberts, in *The Wild Girl*, gave us a fifth gospel, the story of her life with Christ and the disciples told by Mary Magdalene. The fantasy writer Tad Williams is probably best known for his *Memory, Sorrow and Thorn* books, a trilogy that became so large that the third volume was published as two separate books. (Fantasy is nothing if not flexible.) However, his most recent – considerably shorter – novel, *Caliban's Hour*, builds on the stories that were left untold by Shakespeare in *The Tempest*.

The Tempest ends with Prospero giving up his magic, and contemplating retirement once he has given his blessing to his daughter Miranda and the young Ferdinand, whose wedding will be celebrated in Naples. Tad Williams allows Caliban to catch up with Miranda, in Naples, twenty years later. Caliban then tells his story, and the story of his mother, Sycorax. It is a story full of pain and anguish, and shot through with a bitter irony. Sycorax, feared by men as a witch, had her tongue burnt out and was cast adrift in a boat in the last months of her pregnancy. Until the shipwreck and the arrival of Prospero on the Isle, Caliban had no speech, because his mother, able only to grunt, could not introduce him to language. Prospero, Caliban's 'cold father', whom he fears and hates, taught him speech. Caliban's story, then, as he begins to tell it to Miranda, in language learnt from her father, is already rich with the emotional complication of past history.

There are many good stories to be heard from those who are on the sidelines of other people's stories. And it is precisely their being on the sidelines, very often, that helps make their own stories, as is the case with Caliban, so compelling. What secrets do these unspoken lives hold? Karen Joy Fowler's short story about Tonto, 'The Faithful Companion at Forty', carries a dedication to others who are on the sidelines, who only have a bit part to play in other people's stories: 'This one is also for Queequeg, for Kato, for Spock, for Tinkerbell, and for Chewbacca.'

You can find stories at the edges of other stories, and build a plot around them. But you can also borrow whole plots and stories. Literature is full of borrowings. Plots do not have to be original. Tad Williams used a story untold in a Shakespeare play. *The Tempest* itself is generally considered to be one of only two of Shakespeare's plays (the other being *Love's Labour's Lost*) in which the plot is original.

It is what you do with the plot, how you make it serve your aims, that is important. One of the most common plot devices in written and indeed in oral literature is the quest. The heroine or hero, or, if you're not writing in heroic mode, then the protagonist, sets off on a journey in search of something: a fortune, a husband, the Holy Grail, a dragon's hoard, a ring, a crystal, a baby or the secret of immortality. There are ups and downs, conflicts, setbacks; sometimes the quest is successful and sometimes not. Sometimes the idea of success is questioned. Almost invariably, the person who is going on the journey becomes changed by that journey and the adventures that befall her during it (without change, it would become a very boring story). In the end, then, whether the object or secret that is sought is found or not, the quest shifts so that a new, or true, self is found.

The journey is an important element of stories in mythology world wide, in legend and in fairytale and folktale. Think of the stories of Odysseus (one of the prototypes of stories of wandering, questing and homecoming in Western literature); think of another Greek story, that of Orpheus searching for Eurydice. From Europe we have the Grail legend. These stories of knights setting out in search of the Grail have been enormously important. The magic and mystery at the heart of one of the best-known of these stories, that of Sir Gawain and the Green Knight, is the very stuff of fantasy. And from folk and fairytale, think of Hansel and Gretel and their journey into the dark wood, or Jack and his journey up the Beanstalk.

These old stories feed and enrich contemporary fantasy, for fantasy has deep roots in legend and mythology.

Stories can be told and retold in a variety of ways, in different settings, with different characters, in different modes. One of my favourite ghost stories, for example, is 'The Monkey's Paw' by W.W. Jacobs, in which an old couple are given a magical monkey's paw which, they are told, will grant them three wishes. They wish for a sum of money. Soon after, they are offered that exact sum of money as compensation for the death of their beloved only son who, they are informed, has been caught in the machinery at work and hideously mangled to death. They wish for his return to life. That night there is a sinister knocking on the door. They realise he has come back from the grave. The father knows that what lurks in the darkness on the other side of the door is not something they want to see. Before the mother can open the door, the father wishes the son dead again.

This is a scary version of what often appears as a comic tale, in which a little old man, a leprechaun or pixie, appears to a homely, humble couple and offers them three wishes. The husband wishes for a sausage, the wife is so outraged at the waste of a wish that she wishes the sausage to attach itself to the end of his nose, and the final wish is used up getting rid of the sausage. In the comic version the couple are no worse off than they were beforehand, and have possibly gained a little in wisdom. In the horror version they have suffered a grievous, irreversible and permanent loss.

I like this story so much that I used the plot – the granting of three wishes and the consequences attendant on that – in a story I wrote in a series of readers for schools. Rather than a husband / wife central relationship, I had a young girl and her grandmother; rather than a little old man or a monkey's paw, I used a computer game. The point is that these old stories can be adapted and used and re-used, and the central plot, the basic storyline, can usually incorporate all sorts of other elements. In 'The Monkey's Paw', to stick with this example, you will find conflict between the characters, which is an essential ingredient of a gripping story. You will find an exploration of the theme of the power of language and the dangers of articulating your desires. This is a common theme in fantasy. Here, the words are given an extremely powerful magic: life and death, no less, hang upon them. In brief, we are given a dramatic illustration of human greed, folly and overreaching. Not bad for a two or three page long folktale!

Do not hesitate to use tried and tested stories. If these stories speak to you, as a reader, if you respond emotionally to them and feel that they contain truths within the story form that evoke a response in your heart, then these are the stories that you will be able to put things into, that you as a story-teller will be able to get to speak for you.

Let's have a look now at three contemporary fantasy novels, to see how they are plotted, and also to see what other plot elements are carried alongside the basic plot.

Geoff Ryman has drawn on the Epic of Gilgamesh in his novel *The Warrior Who Carried Life*. The Gilgamesh Epic is a Babylonian story, the most extensive versions of which come from the beginning of the first millennium BC (the earliest versions are even older). The Epic is considerably older, then, than the Greek legends that have been so influential on Western literature, and considerably older than the Old Testament stories that are the bedrock of Western art and literature (although many of these, of course, have in-corporated, or assimilated, earlier traditions from Babylonian and Sumerian mythology). After the death of his friend Enkidu, a half-savage giant created by the gods, Gilgamesh sets out on a journey to find the Plant of Immortality. The Plant is stolen by a snake, and Gilgamesh fails his initiation into immortality, but during the course of the quest, and this is a powerful element in Geoff Ryman's compelling contemporary novel, Enkidu's spirit returns to earth and shows to Gilgamesh a vision of the eternal grimness of the land of the dead.

'Cal Cara Kerig was five years old when she saw her mother killed. Her mother was mad, Cara was told, and madness was a disruption of the universe.' From these opening lines we can see that Geoff Ryman's *The Warrior Who Carried Life* is set in a world that is completely different from our own. As we saw at the end of chapter 2, Cara's mother is killed for what is seen as her meddling in men's affairs. Cara, who, like her mother is aware of the threat hanging over the land, tries to warn her family. But she is ignored. Then disaster strikes. All of this happens at the beginning. So the story starts off as a revenge drama, with Cara determined to hunt down and destroy the people who have ruined her life. But it soon becomes much more than that.

The story becomes a retelling of various myths of origin, with Cara stepping out of femaleness into female-and-maleness, becoming a mighty warrior and sorceress, and going down into the depths of hell where she meets the serpent, who is Adam, eats of the apple of Knowledge and brings back to earth the Flower of Immortality.

It could be argued that, when European literature embraced realism in the nineteenth century, its mainstream, in prose works anyway, cut itself off from the roots of story-telling, that is the creation myths of the ancient world, such as Gilgamesh, and from the myths that were later incorporated into Judaeo-Christianity. The mainstream, the nineteenth-century novel, separated itself from the forms of fabulation about good and evil, death, life and immortality, in a way that oriental literatures did not. But those myths live on for us now in fantasy and science fiction. It is perhaps in fantasy and science fiction, in the magic apples and flowers, in the power-holding rings and crystals of the first, and in the scientific experiments, viruses and global computer networks of the second, that the drama of the acquisition of Knowledge still lives. It is in fantasy and science fiction that nowadays we come close to dealing with our own mortality through images of elixirs and cryogenics. It is thus we seek to explore, and re-run, our expulsion from Eden, into sorrow, pain and mortality.

These are old, old stories and while, as I said before, old stories are often the best stories, readers don't necessarily want them in their old old form. If that were the case, we would all be sitting around reading Genesis, or struggling with Gilgamesh and Gawain, or banging our heads over Beowulf. These are all archetypal stories, but who wants to read a story that has archetypes as the main characters? How do you bring them to life? How, really, do you make your characters into people, and throw them into conflicts and adventures that have meaning for us, now, as we move into the twenty-first century?

Take Cal Cara Kerig. The man-woman is an ancient figure, appearing in art and literature in a variety of times and cultures from Tiresias at the gates of Thebes through to Fred/Frederica in Michèle Roberts' novel *Flesh and Blood*. In creation myths, the man-woman is emblematic of unity and a paradisaical time before sexual difference split humanity in two. Geoff Ryman gives us these mythical resonances in his vast warrior figure; he also gives us a living woman, a woman despised and rejected, a woman whose femaleness has been hideously attacked, who is consumed with hatred but who is powerless against the objects of her hatred, and he shows us what she feels:

> She looked down dizzily on an impossibly broad chest. How did a chest like that work, what on earth could fill it? Her whole body felt heavier, yet quicker, more instant: great splayed feet and broad, veined hands. Yet somehow the great bulk was less stubborn or long lasting. Hanging nestled between her legs was something that felt like a small new animal. The thought and feel of it paradoxically excited her, and it began to swell. (*The Warrior Who Carried Life*, p.15)

In that short passage a number of subtle differences are noted, after the initial astonishing difference of size. There is humour and tenderness, and, I would suggest, there is a contemporary consciousness of the possibilities of the interpenetration of male and female, of the blurring of boundaries and a questioning of the construction of gender difference.

Even if you are using the most ancient of stories, you are writing now, and that contemporary consciousness you bring to your writing is an important part of what you write. Which is not to contradict the cautions of Chapter 2 about anachronistic language or transporting Mr and Mrs Mundane into another world.

Geoff Ryman's picture of evil in this novel is one of the most brilliantly horrid portraits I have ever come across. If you are writing about evil people and their evil actions, then you must be prepared to make yourself write convincingly about them. This is not always easy. You will have to dig out your own emotions, your own feelings, your own experience. In the first chapter five-year-old Cara's mother is torn apart by dogs. That is violent. She is torn apart by dogs who have been deliberately set upon her by the men of the village. That, you might think, is evil. But it transpires that that evil pales almost into insignificance (although Ryman is too good a writer to allow that to happen, and the relationship between Cara and her dead mother is one of the important relationships in the story), when we discover in chapter two what it is that Cara's mother foresaw and what the men of her family refused to do anything about. Galo gro Galu, First Son of the Galu, punishes Cara and her family in a scene of quite startling cruelty.

I don't mean by this that the writer must experience this kind of violence before she or he can write about it, of course not. But I am saying that in order to portray evil as horribly realistically as this, you have to be able to imagine not mindless violence, but intelligent, planned, detailed destruction of another person, psychological as well as physical.

It is this that fuels the rage in Cara that in turn fuels the energy to turn herself from a woman nearly destroyed into a powerful male warrior and great sorceress. This consistency is important. So hideous is the punishment meted out against Cara's family that the reader cannot help but want to avenge her pain and hurt with her. But, as noted above, the quest for revenge gives way to other, more complex developments. The secret of the Galu is revealed in a scene that through an eroticisation of evil and the equation of sexual pleasure with death looks forward to the ambivalence of Cara's responses to the choices that face her in the Underworld. It is a strikingly dramatic scene:

> Cara ... thought the Galu did not yet realise he had been struck. Then the Galu stepped towards her on the sword, eyes full of yearning. Stepped forward, and then stepped back. Forward and back, forward and back. Blood welled up into his mouth, and down his chin, and he licked and swallowed it. (*TWWCL* p.49).

The sexualisation of evil in this story is an integral part of the story. For it is a story about sexual difference and mortality. It is a story that appears in the Judaeo-Christian tradition in the form of Adam and Eve and the expulsion from Paradise. And if you are writing that story in the closing years of the twentieth century then can you write it convincingly without allowing the sexual content to appear in the writing?

The struggle between good and evil is not necessarily a straightforward one. Temptation provides many a twist to an ancient plot. Do you remember what Bilbo Baggins does when he escapes from the goblins in the Mountain by squeezing invisible through the crack left by the door? He creeps up on the dwarves and suddenly appears in their midst, to the shame and consternation of Balin, the look-out.

> ... Bilbo was so pleased with their praise that he just chuckled inside and said nothing whatever about the ring ... he sat down and told them everything – except about the finding of the ring ('not just now' he thought). (*The Hobbit*, p.85)

The Hobbit is a precursor of the massive *Lord of the Rings*, and this thread, introduced almost as soon as Bilbo slips the ring into his pocket, this thread of story is there, dramatically, three volumes later, when Gollum in rage and despair and longing leaps up and bites off Frodo's finger and falls to his destruction in the fire at the heart of Mount Doom.

Fantasy may be set in other worlds, it may draw on ancient myths and legends, but good fantasy is always about real people, real feelings, real ambivalences and real conflicts.

This is true of fantasy even in its most stylised form as you will find it in sword and sorcery. For the possibilities inherent in this sub-genre of fantasy writing you could do no better than look at the work of the person who is credited with inventing it, Fritz Leiber, with his long sequence of stories about Fafhrd and the Gray Mouser. Sword and sorcery do not have to be po-faced, nor clichéed; it can be full of fun and ambiguity, tricks and sharpness.

Let's look at the plot of a sword and sorcery novel that I mentioned earlier: by the staggeringly prolific Michael Moorcock. *Elric of Melniboné* is the first in a series, known as the *Elric* saga, of eight novels. Elric is last in a long line of Emperor Sorcerors, ruling over the land of Melniboné, the Dragon Isle, which has ruled the world for ten thousand years but is now decaying. His power is threatened on two sides: from the outside, by the humans of the Young Kingdoms, and from within his court, by his cousin Yyrkoon. The struggle against his cousin Yyrkoon leads him to death and back again, on to other planes of existence, and finally to the magical swords, the runeblades, Stormbringer and Mournblade, which will both save and destroy him and his world. The story of the quest and struggle is told in one paragraph in the prologue, which comes from The Chronicle of the Black Sword, which is, we learn later on, a chronicle of all history that was and is to come.

The story is full of magic, wit and trickery, of deals made and bargains struck. It is full of the richness of old stories, and yet it has a very contemporary feel to it. When Elric makes a pact with Arioch the Lord of Chaos we are reminded of all the deals that have been struck between humans and gods; the elementals of earth and sea that appear in this novel call up any number of creation myths. In order to defeat the Mirror of Memory, Elric sends blind soldiers forward, thus displaying the wit and cunning that are an essential characteristic of our mythical heroes. Think of Odysseus making his sailors plug their ears so as not to hear the sirens' song, while he is strapped to the mast. Or calling out 'Nobody!' in answer to the Cyclops' question: who are you? Elric exemplifies the old story of brain versus brawn. He embodies that old figure, the trickster.

And yet ... this is not an old story, but a modern one. As with Geoff Ryman, Michael Moorcock infuses old, well-tried patterns with a contemporary consciousness. The narrative may be driven by the destiny, or fate, that pulls Elric onwards, but my goodness he is an unwilling hero. He is full of existential angst. As he says at one point: 'I have looked at what I have done, not at what I meant to do or thought I would like to do, and what I have done has, in the main, been foolish, destructive and with little point.'

The characters in this novel have a tendency to speak, or smile, or do whatever it is they are doing, with irony. Elric himself is divided, unsure, sensitive to the ironies of his own fate, not wholly good nor wholly bad, a hybrid creature unable to live up to the hedonism of his forebears and troubled with the human burden of a conscience.

Elric has a peculiarly modern feel to him. This is put most succinctly by Tad Williams, who suggested that Elric is 'the perfect teenage rock-and-roll hero ... skinny, pale, depressed, unlucky in love, but when called upon he can kick major butt.' (interview with Stan Nicholls *Interzone* 91/Jan 95)

And finally, a crossover novel. Barbara Hambly is a popular and prolific American writer of fantasy novels. *The Time of the Dark* is Volume One in the *Darwath Trilogy*. In her dreams Gil, a mediaeval scholar (like Hambly herself once was), slips over into another world in which she sees panic, fear, ruination and something nasty coming up through a hole in the floor. She is recognised as coming from elsewhere by a wizard, Ingold Inglorion, who seeks her help in saving a baby, Altir, the last of the line of Dare, from the forces of darkness, who are otherwise known simply as the Dark. Already you will notice Hambly has perpetrated some of the 'don'ts' of previous chapters: a heroine whose name no one knows how to pronounce (if it was a soft 'g', then why is it not spelled in the normal way, ie 'Gill', but whoever heard of a woman called Gil with a hard 'G'?); a hero wizard with a faintly preposterous name ('Inglorion' has not escaped the critical eye of our Heroic Reader); and perhaps most risky of all, bearing in mind that the standard of proofreading in many major publishing houses has slipped abysmally in the last ten to fifteen years (and more about this in chapter 9), her use of key words that are near-identical: Dar, Dare and Dark. Deliberate, perhaps? Even so, not to be recommended.

However, Hambly is a good storyteller and her expertise allows her to do certain things that a beginning writer would be well advised to avoid. And if I haven't said it already, perhaps now is the time to say that while rules and guidelines are not necessarily 'there to be broken', they nonetheless can be broken and regularly are broken. The more confident and experienced a writer is, the more she, or he, is tempted to bend the rules, to push at the boundaries of the form. And that is as it should be.

The fight between the forces of good and the forces of darkness provides the backbone of Barbara Hambly's novel, and in that it is typical of much contemporary fantasy, or what might be termed 'genre fantasy'. The forces of darkness do not, essentially, change during the course of the book. They start off as sharks of the night, pulling flesh from bones and soul and spirit from the living body, and sharks of the night is what they remain.

Compare this to other kinds of genre stories, such as thrillers and detective novels. Detective novels invariably and thrillers almost always depend for their plots on hidden aspects of people's characters and personalities: very often the good will turn out bad and the bad will turn out good. The skill of detection lies in uncovering, or provoking into self-revelation, the bad beneath the good (or vice versa). The skill of thrilling lies in the exploitation of that profound uncertainty about other people or, in other words, in the unsettling of the trust that we have learned to place in certain other people: the babysitter looked such a sweet old dear, surely she couldn't .... (Even young children respond to this: Mary Rayner's *Mr and Mrs Pig's Evening Out*, featuring Mrs Wolf as the babysitter, is an all-time spooky thriller.) One way or another the writer of thrillers or detective stories will create psychological tension through suspicion and surprise.

In *The Time of the Dark* the suspicions or surprises are to be found amongst the minor rather than the major characters; the tension in the main plot is not psychological. If we know from the beginning who is good and who is bad, how then is the conflict made exciting? The actual clashes, the pitched battles, the chases, the near-captures, are all vividly written but, as I said before, while the conflict between good and bad serves as the backbone, there are various other plot lines that crisscross and interweave and that draw the reader in and keeps her interest.

The more things there are going on, the richer will be the tale, for the more ways there will be of reading it. This does not mean that you have to have a cast of thousands. It is important to remember that your central characters can be in more than one story at a time, just as in real life you yourself are engaged at any one moment in a host of different quests, relationships, dreams and discoveries. In *The Time of the Dark*, alongside the main quest adventure, there are romance stories, family stories (explored through the contrast between Gil's family history and that of the young man Rudy who first becomes involved by chance – or so it seems – and crosses the Void with her), growing old stories, faith and belief stories.

And, finally, as in all crossover stories, there is the very strong storyline that runs like a thread throughout the wanderings in another world: the homecoming. How is your protagonist going to get home? Will she be able to cross the Void without the forces of the Dark following hot on her heels? Will she find the door she came through? When she does return, will home be unrecognisable, as in Rip Van Winkle type stories, and in science fiction that involves suspended animation as our heroes and heroines speed between the stars? Or will only a minute or so have passed in our world, as in the Narnia stories? Will she, or he, want to return home when the time comes? Exile, wanderings in a different land, homecomings and what has happened in one's absence: this is the stuff of myth and dream. Of course this may not be your main storyline, but do not overlook the emotional and literary richness it offers.

At the end of *The Time of the Dark*, Gil and Rudy have not returned to our world. They remain in Darwath. They have both, in one way or another, found themselves. Gil indeed considers that she has found home. But is this really a homecoming? The reader will have to read Volumes Two and Three in order to find out!

Plots don't have to be complicated right at the start. Indeed plots don't have to be complicated at all. There is nothing wrong with a simple plot as long as you create in your reader the desire to carry on reading. But if you want a more complicated plot then you can always complicate it when you are half, or whole way through it.

With a rather wild, though enticing simile, Colin Greenland, author of the fantasy novels *The Hour of the Thin Ox* and *Other Voices*, as well as the space opera *Take Back Plenty* and its sequels, has offered this advice in his column in *Focus*, the BSFA Writers' Magazine:

> Plotting is like sex. Plotting is about desire and satisfaction, anticipation and release. You have to arouse your reader's desire to know what happens, to unravel the mystery, to see good triumph. You have to sustain it, keep it warm, feed it, just a little bit, not too much at a time, as your story goes on. That's called suspense. It can raise desire to a frenzy, in which case you are in a good position to bring off a wonderful climax.

I like the idea of feeding your reader's desire. But he goes on in a more practical vein, and is forced to admit that here the simile breaks down entirely:

> Plotting isn't like sex, because you can go back and adjust it afterwards. Whether you plan your story beforehand or not, if the climax turns out to be the revelation that the mad professor's anti-gravity device actually works, you must go back and silently delete all those flying cars buzzing around the city on page one. If you want to reveal something, you need to hide it properly first.

Whether plotting is or is not like sex, Colin Greenland's advice points to a very important relationship between the writer and what she, or he, has written: what you have written is yours. You can change it, you can chop it up, you can put bits in and take bits out, you can do whatever you like with it. At this stage nobody need know. Do not be nervous of it. If you're not happy with the plot, put in something new and see what repercussions it has. Words are not set in concrete, least of all at this stage when you are still writing them. They are there to be played with, to be pulled and pushed around as the fancy takes you.

And there is another way of looking at it. Your relationship with what you are writing, your involvement with it, do not exist necessarily only on a conscious level. Let yourself be open to subconscious promptings. Many writers find that even something as apparently conscious and rational as plotting, that is, providing causes to produce effects, can work on a subconscious level. Tad Williams, for example, says,

> In my *Memory, Sorrow and Thorn* books I discovered that if I trusted my subconscious, or imagination, whatever you want to call it, and if I made the characters as real and honest as I could, then no matter how complex the pattern being woven, my sub-conscious would find ways to tie it together – often doing things far more complicated and sophisticated than I could with brute conscious effort. I would have ideas for 'nodes', as I think of them – story or character details that have lots of potential connections to other such nodes – and even though I didn't quite understand, I would plunk them in. Two hundred pages later, everything would back-fit, and I'd say, 'Ah, *that's* why I wrote that.' (interview with Stan Nicholls *Interzone* 91, Jan 95)

Every novel or story has more than one level of plot. There is what you might call the deep level: the journey, the quest, the homecoming, the conflict, the growing up. The plots of our own literature, the stories we first heard as children.

And then there is the level at which you, the writer, make it into your own story, with the characters you want to write about, the twists and turns in it that you want (and that, as Colin Greenland says, you can put in at any point you like, or that will be put in by your imagination working at a level below your conscious mind). As you write it, it becomes yours.

I'm going to end this chapter with a poem by Jane Yolen, which I think expresses beautifully the relationship between the teller and the tale.

A Story Must Be Held

A story must be held
tightly in the hand,
fingers cupping the weight of it.
Here is 'Mr Fox',
dark, brooding,
a black rockfall of words
in the centre of my palm.

A story must be held
loosely in the heart,
black stone of it
a second chamber,
the beat of it an echo,
murmuration,
remembrance of a voice.

A story must be held
firmly in the mouth,
a pebble between teeth,
a graveled voice:
'This is the tale of Mr Fox
as it is told in England,
as it is spoke on the moors.'

I shall tell you the tale right now:
with my mouth,
with my heart,
with my hand,
my thumbprint on
a thousand others
already whorled into the stone.

Jane Yolen is a poet and writer of fantasy and science fiction for children and adults. This poem gives us an image of a story that is particularly apt for fantasy, with its roots in tradition, in legend and folklore. She shows that a story is not something new and shiny: rather it is old, old as rock, resonant, deep, used by thousands of others and yet, in each telling, unique.

5
Writing and rewriting

In the chapters previous to this we have looked at what fantasy is, or what it might be, and we have looked at the work of a variety of fantasy writers. We've looked at stories, plots, heroes and heroines, journeys, quests, trials, the forces of good and the forces of evil; we've looked at names and speech and the various ways that you might start thinking about your fantasy world and the various ways you might build on your first ideas.

I shall be looking later at more specific aspects of fantasy, namely children's fantasy, comic fantasy and dark fantasy, but before we home in on these different kinds of fantasy I would like to address the all-important question of the actual process of writing. How do you start? How do you carry on? It seems to me appropriate, in the middle of this book, that we should address this question now and see it as the fulcrum on which the rest lies.

So, the time has come, that dreaded time that comes to all writers, that you have been putting off for as long as possible. Not only have you switched on your computer and sharpened three pencils (the pencils are for the peripheral ideas that come to you as you're tapping away at the keyboard and you would lose your train of thought if you turned away from the word processor for a moment, but if you don't jot these ideas down then you'll lose them forever – always have a pencil to hand, and of course a piece of paper or exercise book); but you have also watered all your indoor plants, including that spider plant up on the top shelf in your bathroom, which if it was sentient would be delighted every time it saw you sharpening your pencils and switching on your computer because it would know it was going to be watered; you have hoovered the stairs and even done the corners with that high-powered sucking attachment you don't normally bother with; you have read tonight's television listings, the radio listings, and the summary of climatic conditions in Europe for the coming week; you have spent some time wondering whether you shouldn't nip out to the post office rather than leaving it till later when it will be more crowded, but with an enormous effort of will you have decided against it; and now you are sitting down with a blank screen in front of you and a blank piece of paper by your side.

Remember what *The Hitch Hiker's Guide* says: 'Don't Panic'.

Everyone has to start somewhere. Once you have written, say, ten pages, you may like to glance back at those beginnings I quoted at the end of chapter 2. You can bet your last bag of dwarves' gold that the authors of those books and stories didn't sit down one fine sunny morning and come out with the opening sequences that now seem such assured first lines.

Writing what you know about: what does this mean?

The process of writing fantasy is no different from the process of writing any other kind of fiction. Some people maintain that you should only write what you know about, but what exactly does that mean? Readers of novels and stories are not merely interested in facts and opinions; they read the newspapers for those. Readers are interested in the truth of the experience, and what it says to them. Ursula Le Guin gives a good example, talking about what experience is (and is not):

> ... experience isn't something you go and get – it's a gift, and the only prerequisite for receiving it is that you be open to it. A closed soul can have the most immense adventures, go through a civil war or a trip to the moon, and have nothing to show for all that 'experience'; whereas the open soul can do wonders with nothing. I invite you to meditate on a pair of sisters, Emily and Charlotte. Their life experience was an isolated vicarage in a small, dreary English village, a couple of bad years at a girls' school, another year or two in Brussels, which is surely the dullest city in all Europe, and a lot of housework. Out of that seething mass of raw, vital, brutal, gutsy Experience they made two of the greatest novels ever written: *Jane Eyre* and *Wuthering Heights*.

A writer has to draw on, or dig up, or mine, or discover, what is inside. Le Guin goes on to say:

> The novelist writes from inside. I'm rather sensitive on this point, because I write science fiction, or fantasy, or about imaginary countries, mostly – stuff that, by definition, involves times, places, events that I could not possibly experience in my own life. So when I was young and would submit one of these things about space voyages to Orion or dragons or something, I was told, at extremely regular intervals, 'You should try to write about things you know about.' And I would say, 'But I do; I know about Orion, and dragons, and imaginary countries. Who do you think knows about my own imaginary countries, if I don't?' ('Talking About Writing', *The Language of the Night*, p.172)

It is only you who knows about the imaginary countries you are setting out to describe. It is only you who can show these countries to other people, to your readers. Where do these countries exist? They will exist on the page, and probably in the process of getting them on to the page they will change from your original conception of them, but at the moment, as you face the blank screen and the blank page, they exist only inside you. Whether you prefer to think of them as existing in your imagination, or your heart, or your mind, or indeed your soul, is really only a question of how you prefer to think about these things. What is incontrovertible is that they exist somewhere in there. So how do you reach them to bring them out?

First, you must be open. Be open to your unconscious, listen to your own dreams (as Freud said, dreams are the royal road to the unconscious) and your own nightmares. Search your own memories and try to explore and pursue your own desires and your own fears. It is through your own emotions that you will be able to provide a bedrock of emotional truth for the characters in your imagined world.

Finding the way down to your fantasy world

So how do you do this? Well, there is no easy way. Whoever said writing was easy? First, however, you must allow yourself the time and the emotional or psychological space for this inward journey. Many of your memories, the memories and experiences that are going to feed into and enrich your fantasy world are so deeply buried that they will not immediately or easily come to the surface. You must allow them the time to do that. This can be done in conjunction with the discipline of sitting at your desk for however many hours a day as is needed, and as is possible. Not everybody has eight hours a day to spend at a desk: some people have only an hour or two a day, and that often late at night, when the kids have been put to bed and the washing up done. And maybe the last thing you want to do is go and sit on your own at a desk and write your fantasy story. Maybe watching telly seems easier (which it is) and more appealing. But the discipline of writing for a regular period every day is important.

If you write every day, then every day it is that much easier to step out and onto the royal road, to break through the daily cares and concerns that occupy and sometimes seem to fill the conscious mind almost entirely. If you write every day, then every day you have what you have written the previous day there on the screen or on the page, there to start you off.

Some writers like to stop their day's writing in the middle of their creative flow; stopping mid-paragraph or even sometimes mid-sentence. Finishing that stream of thought or image or idea is what gets them going the next day. Some writers like to read over what they have written the day before, and get an impetus from that to carry them on. Some like to revise and rework what they wrote the day before.

There is no one correct method, no way that suits everyone. Writing methods are as individual, as varied, as writing styles.

Exercises

I am now going to suggest two writing exercises, which are designed to help unlock the doors into those recesses of the heart or imagination where the fuel for your fantasy world is stored. Again, not all exercises work for everyone, and you may find other ones appropriate for yourself, but the couple I am going to suggest have always elicited a good response from the students I have done them with. By good response I mean that the students have been marvellously surprised by what they discovered, by what seemed to flow out from inside them.

The first exercise was invented by Michèle Roberts and appears in a collection of pieces by writers and editors called *Taking Reality by Surprise: Writing for Pleasure and Publication*, edited by the writer Susan Sellers, which is an extremely helpful book packed full of ideas for aspiring and established writers. It includes exercises and advice for all the different stages of writing. Susan Sellers divided the pieces into three sections: Beginnings, with sub-sections on starting, freeing the imagination, finding a subject, finding a voice and openings; Continuings, with sub-sections on genres, keeping the momentum going and writing skills; and Endings, with sub-sections on finishing and publication. You may find that you may not need writing exercises to help get you going or to help you over awkward places or when you are stuck, but if you do, then there are plenty in this book. It is aimed primarily at women writers, but men who are aspiring writers too would get a lot from it.

Sound over sense exercise
This is the first of the two exercises. Think of three language sounds that give you pleasure, and write them down. Then embody the sounds in as many words as you can, or as you feel like. Then write three or four or five sentences using *all* the words. (e.g. your sounds might be 'ush', 'ock' and 'eeze', and the words might include 'hush', 'rush hour', 'luscious', 'frock', 'grockle', 'socket', 'breeze', 'frieze', 'easy' ,etc.) The aim of this exercise is to allow yourself to write sentences that are sound-led rather than sense-led. To place hearing above thinking. To explore the sensual pleasure of speaking and hearing words that include sounds you like. You should say the words out loud and the sentences out loud. Let the pleasure you have found seep into the language or languages that are spoken in your fantasy world. Listen to the pattern the sounds make; you will find a rhythm there that has come from somewhere inside you. Remember that all spoken language has an internal rhythm. If the language spoken in your fantasy world has an internal rhythm it will sound natural, and therefore authentic.

Parts of the body exercise
Allocate yourself a part of the body and let that part speak in the first person. Allow it a monologue, or a rant, or a complaint or a celebration. You could choose fingers, for

example, or stomach (or if you are doing this exercise on your own, rather than in a group where there might be embarrassment, of course you could choose more intimate parts of the body). Say you choose fingers: let them speak about what they do: how every day they are soaked in water and detergent, grazed and roughened as they grip pan scourers; almost worn out by tap tap tapping on a keyboard; how they stroke a beloved's skin, smooth the hair of a sleeping child. Stick to the first person: 'I feel, touch, etc. ...'

If your characters do not exist physically in your fantasy world, they will convince no one. You, the writer, must exist physically in your fantasy world in order for your characters to do so. You must know what it is like to ride a headstrong horse over a mountain pass and have the skin rubbed off your fingers by the double reins; you must know what it is like to be so hungry that the day-old remains of a boiled-up blubber fish rejected even by goblins appear attractive, if not tasty; you must know what it is like to huddle in a cave that is so smoke-filled that your eyes are streaming tears and yet you dare not go outside because if you do ...

Of course, you don't actually have to have done these things, but you have to find within you the belief that you have. You have to listen to the experiences of your own body. This is the case with all writing, but is perhaps particularly so with fantasy, partly because instinct is more important than intellect when it comes to fantasy, but also because a world cannot exist convincingly unless it is physically there and your characters are physically interacting with it. It is no good creating a world of strange and wondrous beauty or fierce and savage primitivism if your characters act as if they have just wandered in from a semi-detached suburban residence and are on their way to collect a takeaway pizza before settling down for an evening in front of the telly.

You must let their bodies speak.

How do other writers do it?

How did other writers get started? How do they carry on? To what extent do they inhabit the worlds they have created? Everyone is different, of course, but it is always interesting to see how other writers deal with the problems you yourself may be facing. Let's look now at what some of the writers, whose work is discussed elsewhere in this book, have to say about different aspects of their art.

Here is Tanith Lee, talking about being the instrument of her story:

> As a writer my means – I can hardly say method – is to allow the story, its nuances, characters, purpose, to shape themselves. I am the instrument. This evidently supposes that I do not, save rarely, interfere during the stages of production. And, when writing in the first person, I become, as an actor does, the character her- or himself.
>
> Why or how one is able to do this, those who can are rarely able to explain. I am inclined to believe myself that it is an avenue open to everyone of reasonable intelligence and sympathy. Not merely to understand – but to become, if only for a moment, another person, regardless of sex, origin or creed, renders to us a compassion of a form for which there is no proper word. But too it gives into our hands valuable weapons of insight and thought. These rewards may not last, but at least we shall have had a brief possession of them.

She goes on to talk about writing in the character of someone who is totally different from herself, the author:

> If writing as a man, then, I do not recall in any way that I am a woman. I am able to put down what my character feels and knows. And drawing back, in the intervals, I have been occasionally shocked at what I have been party to. That does not mean, however, that I would deny a single word. Far from it. I am not a censor, but a recorder. My passion for what, as a writer, I can do, is bound up for ever in my faith that even the fiction I write is real, in some inexpressible way. (*Women as Demons*, introduction, pp.x–xi)

'Even the fiction I write is real.' This is the paradox of good writing. This is why a phrase like 'write what you know about' doesn't make sense unless you investigate that word 'know'. When Tanith Lee writes as a man, then she knows, throughout the time that she is writing, what it is to be a man. Because, for that period of time, she *is* one.

A very different approach is that taken by Ramsey Campbell, talking here about his *very* early writing career. Ramsey Campbell began by imitating his favourite author, H.P. Lovecraft, and here, in an article in *The Author* entitled 'My First Book' he bravely invites us to enjoy the fruits of his imitation:

'No sign of life was discernible inside (the house), and outside the garden was filled with a brooding quiet, while my shadow on the fungus-overgrown lawn appeared eldritch and distorted, like that of some ghoul-born being from nether pits.'

Campbell resolutely refuses to let Lovecraft take the blame:

Lovecraft very seldom wrote like that, and imitators such as myself are to blame for a persistent notion that he always did. Even I can't claim to have perpetrated much writing quite as, er, spectacular as this telegram later in the same story, 'The Tomb-Herd':

'To Richard Dexter. Come at once to Kingsport. You are needed urgently by me here for protection from agencies which may kill me – or worse – if you do not come immediately. Will explain as soon as you reach me ... But what is this thing that flops unspeakably down the passage towards this room? It cannot be that abomination which I met in the nitrous vaults below Asquith Place ... IA! YOGSOTHOTH! CTHULHU FHTAGN!'

Well, I was only fourteen. (*The Author*, Spring 1995)

Perhaps it was only seldom that Lovecraft wrote like that, although it seems to me that ridiculous though these pieces are in some way, they do have a passion in them (OK, a fourteen year old's passion, but passion nonetheless) which sets them apart already from the wooden prose and wooden emotions of many a published writer; nonetheless the second piece does illustrate a peculiarly Lovecraftian problem: if the unspeakably flopping abomination is heading fast down the passage towards you, why on earth are you sitting at your desk writing about it rather than scrambling out the window and racing off like a bat out of hell? Well, Lovecraft's narrators were often fated to meet up finally with the abomination. They knew there was no escape for them: but they knew it was their duty to future generations to transcribe faithfully every ghastly step leading up to the final horror, when the pen slips from the fear-frozen fingers and leaves a trail of ink across the page. But how come the manuscript was found and published? Different writers use different framing devices: Edgar Allan Poe had a manuscript found in a bottle ('At the last moment I will enclose the MS in a bottle, and cast it within the sea'), Arthur Conan Doyle had his Dr Watson at hand to write everything down, stories are told at second or third hand, or, if the narrator doesn't actually meet his or her death, can be recollected in tranquillity and then transcribed. This problem – how do you get first person immediacy and authenticity ('what is this thing that flops unspeakably ... ?') if that person is no longer around to tell the tale? – is not restricted to genre fiction: think of the endless letters found, or memoirs unearthed, in mainstream and literary fiction. Writers and readers enter into a pact: readers are willing to believe all that the writer of fiction makes up, on condition that they are not asked to believe something totally ridiculous. With a ghost story, or any kind of tale of the uncanny, you must think of how the story came into your possession.

As Ramsey Campbell learned, 'CTHULHU FHTAGN!' isn't good enough. Possibly, and I'm speculating here, it might have taken him longer to learn if he hadn't actually been writing the stuff himself.

Not all writers believe that imitation is helpful when you are learning to write. But it is worth remembering that before you have discovered your own voice – and it is a rare writer who does not have to work towards that discovery – the chances are high that you are imitating someone else anyway, unconsciously. There is something to be said for consciously doing what you would otherwise do unconsciously, and writing is a craft like any other, with techniques to be tried, even if you later reject them.

A perceptive publisher realised that the Lovecraftian influence needed leavening. August Derleth of Arkham House (Lovecraft's first publishers) encouraged Ramsey Campbell, and offered useful advice by suggesting: '"for the improvement of your literary form, that you vary your reading of Lovecraft with an extensive reading of the ghost stories of M.R. James, whose leisurely approach served to fix his settings and his ghosts so memorably in the reader's imagination". The rest of his advice,' says Ramsey Campbell '– to relocate the tales in the Severn Valley, to show events rather than report them, to have the characters speak (like real people, he might have added) energised me no end, so much so that the first new tale I wrote might as well have been the work of a different, and certainly better, writer.'

And after that, it was a question of working and reworking, and struggling on even when confidence was low:

Having learned some craft by imitation, in my view the best method, I set about sounding like myself. I was now reading far more widely, and wanted to bring themes I found in the main-stream into my own stuff. Graham Greene's technique came as a revelation, and in particular Nabokov's use of language. I spent five years on my second published book: two and a half years writing the first drafts of half a dozen stories, which I then used to show myself how not to write the tales. I rewrote them from scratch, teaching myself in the process the way to write the rest of the book, and at last typed up the handwritten material, seventy thousand words or so. I vividly remember staring at the typescript and being overcome by a conviction which had inter-mittently troubled me; that if nobody else was writing super-natural fiction like mine, everyone else in the field was right and I was wrong. It took me a while to summon up the enthusiasm to post the typescript of *Demons by Daylight* to Derleth. .... On the basis of one long and highly favourable review I decided to write full-time. But that's a comedy for another occasion.

Tanith Lee and Ramsey Campbell are two of the fifty writers (of fantasy, science fiction and horror) who are interviewed about their work by Stan Nicholls in his book *Wordsmiths of Wonder*. The other writers include (and these are the ones whose work I have referred to or will refer to) Robert Holdstock, Michael Moorcock, Terry Pratchett, Michael Swanwick, Lisa Tuttle and Tad Williams. The writers all speak openly and interestingly about their work, and there is much to encourage the beginning writer. Michael Swanwick, for example, recounts how for the first ten years of his writing life he never managed to finish a single story. Reading other writers on their work can give you a sense of community, can helpfully make you feel that your problems are not unique. And for similar reasons you should join the British Science Fiction Association (as open to those interested in fantasy as in SF) or the British Fantasy Society (which in the past has tended to be dominated by the dark fantasy/horror side of fantasy.)

Writing is in some ways a gift and it is always hard graft. It is the most subtle and effective means of communication, and yet it is deeply lonely. It requires passion, and perseverance, and faith. And after all of that, you've still probably got to rewrite the pesky thing ...

Revising and rewriting

You have typed 'ends' and done your word count. That's it, you think, finished, time for a celebratory drink. And in all probability you deserve one. But after that it's back to your manuscript, which is not your finished manuscript but is a draft. It may be a draft that is very similar to what the finished manuscript is going to be, but even so it is still a draft.

When an editor considers your work, you want her, or him, to think that the way you have put the words on the page is the only possible way that the words could be there. They are the only possible words that could have been used to describe what you are describing.

Many beginning writers, in my experience, are loth to make cuts and changes in what they have written because they feel it is so much a part of themselves. They feel, perhaps, that to admit to a weakness anywhere is to undermine the whole edifice. If one part isn't good enough to keep in, they think in panic, who is to say that maybe all the other parts are no good as well.

You must overcome this feeling. You have just finished writing a work of fiction and that in itself is no mean feat: it has required of you patience, perseverance, determination and the ability to sit on your own for long periods of time communing only with what is inside your own head. Take courage and confidence from that.

Remember: it is you who control the language, not the language which controls you. And anyway, if you are obliged to cut out a sizeable chunk from the middle of your novel, it doesn't mean that it is lost forever. You may be able to use it in another novel or story; or it may be that you needed to put that in while you were writing to enable you to get to the heart of something, and now that you have got to the heart of whatever it is, you don't actually need the steps that took you there.

It is not easy to edit your own work, but it is a necessary skill. Once you are an established writer an agent might fulfil the role of first, and critical, reader, or if you are lucky enough to be published by a publishing house that still employs an old-fashioned editor who sees it as her job to read and comment and make suggestions, you will have an editor who does that. But when you start out you have only yourself, your doting Mum and other beginning writers.

First, discount your doting Mum. And any other family member, such as sensitive spouse ('How come evil Lord – or Lady – W'ggleb'rd has blue eyes? I've got blue eyes, so I hope you haven't based him on me, you B'st'rd.'), or brutal ('Do you want me to be *really* honest?') brother. Members of your own family read too much into fiction, looking for themselves or looking for part of you, and then being hurt or offended by what they find (or don't find) there. You don't need to be distracted by justifying to your family members what you have or haven't put into your fiction.

However, there is nothing better than being made to justify, by other writers, what you have written. Other writers can say to you: why have you spent three pages on a description of the banqueting hall when all the action takes place in the throne room? Why have you used first person narration? Why have you described your heroine as sloe-eyed on the first page and doe-eyed on the second, and what do you mean anyway by either, or both, of those terms? And so on. Other writers do not have a personal axe to grind with you. They are interested in the writing.

So, if at all possible, find yourself a writing group. Apply for a place on a Creative Writing course, of which there are increasing numbers. Find out if any of the writers you admire are teaching for the Taliesin or Arvon Trusts, and apply for their courses. Being on a creative writing course does not mean that you will be taught how to write a successful book, but it means that you will be given support and encouragement with your writing and perhaps most importantly it will give you a group of similar minded people who will take your writing seriously as writing and who will act as a first audience. The experience of having other people listen to your work and the experience of listening critically to other people's work, help foster the necessary distance required between yourself and the words you have written. It is not easy to be objective about your own work but, when you are reworking and revising something you have written, the more objective you can be, the better. If you cannot find a local group of other writers then you have only yourself as first audience. It is helpful to read what you have written out loud. Reading aloud to yourself reveals the rhythm of your words. Unconscious repetitions are much more more easily noticed when spoken aloud. Everyone – even famous writers – has favourite words, or indeed phrases, that it is hard not to over use. (I can think of one widely published and extremely good author who has a thing about the phrase 'infinite care'). With dialogue, you will be able to hear better, through hearing them spoken aloud, whether a character's speech patterns are consistent or not. And, when they are spoken aloud, it is much easier to spot unnoticed ambiguities in the words. Sentences such as 'He leant over and stroked her soft calf' (rather than her newly born calf?) or 'She sat down on a rent sofa' (next to a rent boy, perhaps?) should not slip through the editorial, or self-editorial, net.

Every sentence counts. Why bother to write, otherwise?

The first step then is to get your work listened to. The next step is to get your work into print. We will be looking at that hurdle in chapter 9, but before then I would like to look at the different types of fantasy you may be interested in. So we will leave the general rules for the moment and come back to them later when we consider publication. Now let us look at three very healthy areas of fantasy: children's fantasy, comic fantasy and dark fantasy.

6
Children's fantasy

All good children's fantasy can be read with enjoyment by adults. Perhaps this is because writers of children's fantasy do not write for children as an audience out there but write for the child inside themselves. Perhaps it is worth thinking about that a bit more: many of what are now considered to be classics of children's literature – almost all of them with elements of fantasy in them if not wholly fantasies – stay with people throughout their lives. This is undoubtedly partly to do with reading them, or having them read to one, at an early and impressionable age, at an age when the imagination is plastic and flexible, at an age when impressions leave a deep imprint. But it is also to do with what they deal with and with the way that they express profound fears and hopes and dreams.

Adult readers often want nice and complex stories for full satisfaction, but children don't. Children don't need complexity, but they do need emotional and imaginative depth and so the images in children's literature often carry a weight of meaning. They must be strong, clear and simple, not muddy and mixed up. Think about how images from so-called children's literature haunt you in a way that those from adult books often don't (adult books perhaps are too concerned with the subtleties of argument and relationships).

Different people remember different bits of the classics best, and will remember them after fifty years or more. From Edith Nesbit's *Five Children and It*, for example, I remember not just the grumpy old Psammead with its aversion to water but I particularly remember the chapter in which the children grow wings and then become stuck on top of the tower as night falls. That yearning for wings: to be able to fly, as a child, was to be free of all the constraints – physical and mental – of being a child. To be able to fly, as an adult, is also to be free.

This explains my soft spot for winged horses, dragons and other fantastical creatures.

I also remember from *Five Children and It*, and from Edith Nesbit's Bastable books (*The Treasure Seekers* and so on), and from *The Railway Children*, the strong impression that I was reading about children who were alone in the world and were making sense of the world on their own. They were discovering their own strengths and the powers of their imaginations to create things, without the help or intervention of adults. In a way that as far as I remember was not clearly spelled out but was nonetheless clear as daylight, these children had lost their parents. Not that their parents were dead. They were simply not there. The writer Diana Hendry has suggested that 'in children's books there are a lot of lost/dead/missing parents because the child's imaginative world is shut off from the adult world.' She goes on: 'Mine was! Certainly I didn't communicate to my parents that I thought there was a left-over Nazi living on the sandhills or that the sweet shop at the top of the high street was run by a witch or that the tree that tapped at my window at night was trying to get in ...'

Furthermore, separation – whether through death or some other form of loss (in fiction this might be represented as a parent imprisoned, or lost in some other way) is an integral part of growing up; that is, in order to grow up, you have to separate yourself from your parents. And with separation comes the development of memory and the growth of the transforming power of the imagination. It is not surprising then that the best children's writers draw upon their own memories when they write, whether it is consciously or unconsciously, and transform them in the process of writing.

If I say that it is important for children's writers to write about themselves, I do not mean that they should write autobiography. I mean that they should write out of the emotional experiences that have stayed with them since they were children, those profound experiences that shape us all and stay with us all. Such writers will place the subjective experience of the child at the centre of the book, rather than taking up the position of grown-up author writing for (or down to) the child.

These comments do not apply only to fantasy writing, but to writing for children in general, just as in the previous chapter much of what was said about the process of writing was applicable to writing any form of fiction.

Anybody who wishes to embark on writing fantasy for children would be well advised to read Margaret Clark's invaluable *Writing for Children*. Margaret Clark is a highly experienced editor of children's books. On the very first page of her introductory chapter she says that 'it is important to remember, at the outset, that writing for children requires no less skill with words than writing for anyone else.' This is as true of fantasy as it is of any other kind of writing. She also makes the point that there is no one way of writing for children, 'any more than there is one way of writing a book for adults, and', she goes on, 'for the children's writer it is vital to find your own voice from the start.' Why? Because children are novice readers, and if you don't entice and excite and enthral them at the beginning of your story, with a distinctive voice that will capture their attention, then they won't (unlike some – although not all – adult readers) give you the benefit of the doubt. They will simply stop reading.

In the section on fantasy, Margaret Clark emphasises the need to make your world inviting to the reader, internally consistent and yet not totally dependent on the setting at the expense of the story. She describes her regret at having to reject manuscripts of novels that had been written with painstaking care but in which it was obvious that 'the writer had become so preoccupied with this other world that all the creative energy had gone into its loving construction, with not much thought left for the purpose of it all.' This overemphasis on setting is to be avoided by writers with adult readers in mind as much as by those who are writing for children. If you find you are beginning to spend more time on your map than on your story – then watch out! But it is especially important in writing for children, again perhaps because children are less experienced readers than adults, not to sacrifice the story to the setting. This is not to say that fantasy writing for children must be action packed, or intricately plotted; simply that the shape must be carefully thought about.

One of the examples that Margaret Clark uses in her section on teenage novels is a fantasy novel that incorporates many of the aspects of fantasy already discussed. Alan Garner's *The Owl Service* draws on old legend – it is taken from a story in the Welsh *Mabinogion* – as an integral part of the plot. The mythical story is interwoven with a present-day drama. Times and places cross and overlap, and there is movement between the worlds. This is a crossover novel, written in a highly charged, poetic style. What makes it a novel for children, then? The main characters are two adolescent boys and a girl, but that in itself doesn't make it a novel for adolescents. Think of Henry James' *The Turn of the Screw*, or *What Maisie Knew*, which are hardly books for children. Alan Garner occupies a rather odd position in the pantheon of classic children's writers, for many people now consider him not to be 'really' a children's writer at all. Certainly his notoriously 'difficult' novel *Red Shift* is more and more often referred to as an adult book, and some critics, such as Lisa Tuttle, suggest that the widely acknowledged awkwardnesses of his powerful first novel *The Weirdstone of Brisingamen* arise precisely from the fact that it is not a children's book at all, but that he made it into a children's book because back then, in the early 1960s, if you were writing fantasy then you were a children's writer, no question. *The Owl Service* won a major children's book prize – the Carnegie Medal – in 1967 and also the *Guardian* children's book award. But then it was well reviewed on the adult books page of *The Sunday Times* and nobody could get hold of it in a library because it had been classified (in the British National Bibliography) as J for Juvenile, that is, for the under fourteens.

Until the late 1960s there were books for children (under fourteens) and there were books for adults. So readers of fourteen, fifteen, sixteen, seventeen, eighteen, were out in the cold, even although there were marvellous novels, like *The Owl Service*, ideally suited to that age group. But what teenager would willingly go to library shelves that were classified as suitable for under-fourteens?

In the late 1960s Aidan Chambers, teacher and ghost-story writer and compiler of many excellent dark fantasy/ghost anthologies, was campaigning vigorously at the time that his book *The Reluctant Reader* was published for separately published fiction for readers of secondary school age. There is now a thriving teenage market, and with that has come a blurring of the boundaries between adult and children's fiction, and perhaps in particular, between adult and children's fantasy. Fantasy appeals across the age groups in a way that, for example, thrillers or detective stories do not. Is this perhaps to do with the roots of fantasy lying in an oral tradition in which the storyteller told her tales to an audience of children and adults together?

I started this chapter by suggesting that all good fantasy written for children can be read with pleasure by an adult. I think I might mention here there is also good fantasy written for adults that can be enjoyed by children. Terry Pratchett springs to a mind as an excellent example of this. I will be talking about Terry Pratchett later, but he is worth mentioning here as a writer who slips easily across markets. His *Discworld* novels are adult novels, highly sophisticated in terms of language and literariness, but as everybody knows twelve year olds just love them.

There is an enormous range of fantasy writing for children, and there is a parallel wide range of ways in which fantasy books are marketed. Fantasy, it must be said, plays an important part in all writing for children. Readers, however, (and buyers – not necessarily the same people when you're considering children's books) seem to have different perceptions of it and publishers market their children's books in very different ways.

As a means of illustrating the wide range available I'm now going to look at three contemporary children's novels. They will show not just what themes are dealt with in contemporary children's fantasy, but how those themes are dealt with and, very importantly, how such books are marketed. I have chosen three books that seem to be aimed (primarily) at the young teenage market. The publishers expect them to be read mainly by children aged between eleven and sixteen. Yet although the publishers are going for one fairly closely defined market, the way these books are presented to the potential reader/buyer varies considerably.

Let's consider: *The Awesome Bird* by Diana Hendry, *Black Unicorn* by Tanith Lee and *Redwall* by Brian Jacques (Volume One of the *Redwall* trilogy).

The Awesome Bird has a basically simple story within and around which the author manages to raise a variety of complex questions, not all of which, by any means, are answered. The book describes two worlds. In the Other World, on the Island where the Rabobab lives, dreams are made and songs are sung that feed the dreams and songs, the hopes, desires and imaginations, of the Worldly World and those who live in it. The Awesome Bird, which Laurie, who only knows small city birds, mistakes for a snowy owl at the beginning of the story, ferries the Island children to and from the Worldly World. These children must go there to gather material for their dreams and songs. But something goes wrong and the Awesome Bird takes Laurie, the wrong child, back to the Island.

Will Laurie be rescued in time by his mother and beloved dog Puddles, before the sea washes away all his memories of his life before?

There are many fantasy elements in this novel: flying on the back of a bird (in other books you might find a dragon, or a winged horse) to another world; the quest element (what is wrong with the Awesome Bird, and who is the Rabobab?); the crossover, or two world setting, which raises the question of where home really is. It echoes the lost boys of *Peter Pan* not just in the children of the Island living without parents or other adults organising them, but in the loss of and longing for mothers.

Diana Hendry's previous novel *Harvey Angell* also has strong fantasy elements. Harvey Angell himself is an electrician from elsewhere, here in this world only temporarily, in order to connect up broken circuits of loving relationships. Diana Hendry has said that in fantasy she has discovered parts of herself that she did not know were there. So there is a strong personal element in these books that gives them depth and resonance. It gave her access, she has said, to 'deep and strong emotions that are hard to reach – or perhaps face – in any other way. They are like the truths sometimes presented to us in dreams.'

Harvey Angell won the 1991 Whitbread Award, Children's Section (the overall Award has never been given to the winner of the Children's Section). Diana Hendry is a poet and her poetic approach to language is reflected in her prose style and in the concerns she explores in her novels. Both *Harvey Angell* and *The Awesome Bird* look at loss and love and healing, and *The Awesome Bird* in particular expresses the power and importance of dreams, songs and the life of the imagination.

Diana Hendry suspects that

> ... to write fantasy for children you have to put yourself in a
> rather odd state of mind. I suspect it's necessary to switch off
> part of the rational mind and this is quite hard to do. During the
> first draft of *The Awesome Bird*, the rational me would intervene
> every now and again and say 'this is preposterous!' It's hard to
> trust to the story, but I believe that's what you have to do. It's a

curious kind of balance between the conscious and the unconscious mind.

A bit like riding a horse, she suggests: 'You have to ride and control it and stay on its back, but it's the horse that knows where it's going. For after all, it's a magic horse!'

Neither of these books is marketed as or seen as genre 'fantasy'. Their style and presentation say: literary books for children and young adults.

In adult publishing nowadays, with the role of the individual editor being sacrificed to the demands of the marketing department, editors are increasingly unwilling or unable (that is, not allowed) to take on cross-genre books. Books that aren't easily labelled as one thing or another (unless of course you're so well known that books will sell on your name alone. Who says Jeffrey Archer doesn't write fantasy?) seem to strike fear into the hearts of publishers.

But fantasy is accepted as a part of writing for children. It is seen as perfectly normal. And so a prestigious prize like the Whitbread can go to a novel that includes strong elements of fantasy. If you are writing for children you don't need to go searching for the obscure door at the dark end of the corridor that says: Fantasy Editor.

Very different in presentation from *The Awesome Bird* is Tanith Lee's *Black Unicorn*, which has 'Winner of the World Fantasy Award' in big letters on the cover. This is a coming-of-age story, and as such has a distinct appeal to the teenage market, but it can be read with great pleasure by an adult. Lee never talks down, and puts as much passion and poetry into her writing for young people as into her other books and stories. Lee is extraordinarily prolific, and seems at ease in all lengths: short stories, novellas, single novels and series. She is notable for the richness of her imagery and the down-to-earthness of many of her observations. There is a humour to her writing which is very appealing. The heroine of *Black Unicorn* is bored sulky adolescent Tanaquil, who is accompanied on all her adventures by a small talking animal called a peeve which can be distinctly – well – peevish. During the course of the story Tanaquil separates herself from her sorceress mother, finds and then turns her back on her father and discovers her own abilities. Tanaquil thinks she has no magical abilities at all, but it is she who hears the music of the unicorn's bones, she who hears the night wind wrapped round its horn. It is she who brings the bones of the unicorn to life. Tanaquil is quickwitted, brave, generous and loving – and this feisty fare for young readers is part of a story that has moments of magical beauty.

Despite the book's obvious appeal to the young adult market, *Black Unicorn* is presented as mainstream genre fantasy, with gilt letters for the title on the cover and all the trimmings, including a quote from *Asimov's*. But then perhaps this is because young adults make up quite a large proportion of the readership of fantasy anyway.

There are some obvious differences between writing fantasy for children and writing fantasy for adults. There are certain areas that must be dealt with carefully: sexuality, death, violence, for example. In her book Margaret Clark talks about these 'danger zones', and the attitudes and assumptions that are apparent – or not so apparent – in contemporary children's publishing. However, the best way of finding out what is and is not acceptable is to look at the literature yourself. You may be surprised. For example, there is probably more violent death in children's fantasy than some adults expect.

Redwall, for example, starts off with some very charming scenes of mice and other animals, not unlike the Brambly Hedge picture books, but after barely ten pages a rat called Skullface is forced by his master Cluny the Scourge to leap onto the back of a bolting horse and bite it to make it go faster:

> Skullface had time for just one agonized scream before he fell. The iron-shod cartwheels rolled over him. He lay in a red mist of death, the life ebbing from his broken body. The last thing he saw before darkness claimed him was the sneering visage of Cluny the Scourge roaring from the jolting back-board, 'Tell the devil Cluny sent you, Skullface!' (p.27)

Which is not to say that the violence is what makes *Redwall* popular with younger readers! Part of its appeal at least lies in the wonderful descriptions of feasting at the Abbey, as here when the young novice mouse Matthias has caught a fully grown grayling for the night's feast:

> ... course after course was brought to the table. Tender fresh-water shrimp garnished with cream and rose leaves; devilled barley pearls in acorn puree, apple and carrot chews; marinated cabbage stalks steeped in creamed white turnip with nutmeg.

> A chorus of oohs and aahs greeted the arrival of six mice
> pushing a big trolley. It was the grayling. Wreaths of aromatic
> steam drifted around Cavern Hole; it had been baked to perfec-
> tion... (p.24)

What a wonderfully cosy pleasant scene it is, made all the
more so by the knowledge that heading towards the Abbey,
bent on torture, enslavement and massacre, is the evil, one-
eyed Cluny the Scourge.

Redwall, like *Black Unicorn*, has a mass market look to it: the
gilt letters call out to the potential buyer: come buy, I am
popular. The cover of the Red Fox edition, illustrating the evil
Cluny with his rat horde, suggests to adult buyers that it
would be suitable for younger readers (it is obviously a book
about animals), while to the younger buyer or browser, it
says: adventure and excitement.

Interestingly, the wild-eyed frightened horse on the cover
of *Redwall* is not unlike the unicorn on the Orbit edition of
Black Unicorn. A rearing horse (with or without single horn) is
an instantly recognisable fantasy image.

In recent years there has been a critical tendency against
fantasies that feature animals in clothes, that is, animals acting
in human ways. It is seen as being too cosy, too Beatrix
Potterish and old-fashioned. But the *Redwall* books are very
popular: they are not at all cosy or old-fashioned, and they
depict a wide range of human behaviour, from the virtues of
loyalty, generosity, courage and honour, through to the vices
of greed, stupidity, overweening ambition and just plain old
love of mindless violence. Jacques creates some delightfully
observed minor characters: the mad King of the sparrows, the
shrews with their endless trade union style debates, Julian
Gingivere the aristocratic cat and his one-time friend Captain
Snow the old bufferish owl. He creates a story that allows
these characters to act in ways that amuse, entertain and, in
some instances, move the reader. There is a delightful scene
with Matthias, Methuselah the oldest mouse in the Abbey,
and Constance the badger as they set off on the first step of
the solemn quest to discover the hiding place of the sword of
the fabled Martin the Warrior. They are teasing each other,
laughing and making merry. Yet in no time at all Methuselah,
who as you would expect from his name is not only kind and
gentle but is also old and wise, is killed casually, accidentally,
by a mindless young thug of a fox.

'Dying,' says Brian Jacques, 'is a part of life. I would hate to write a book where all the goodies stay alive. Life isn't like that.' It is this realism that gives the fantasy world its credibility. In *Redwall* a bitter war is fought for the Abbey, and in any war there has to be violence and death. Although the animals speak, they are not cartoon characters, but creatures of fur, flesh and feather, prone to ageing, vulnerable to violence. Not, in other words, invincible or immortal. They are imagined in their physicality despite their human attributes, and placed firmly within a realistically drawn English countryside. Setting is an important part of fantasy: both countryside (here, and in Robert Holdstock's work as previously mentioned) and contemporary urban landscapes (as in Ramsey Campbell's work), provide richness, variety, you might even say a heartland out of which the fantasy grows.

But of course Brian Jacques is not showing death simply because it is 'a part of life'. He is showing it in a particular way that will allow the younger reader to make sense of it. Throughout the centuries literature and art have struggled to offer meanings to the mysteries of life. 'If you love a person,' says Brian Jacques, 'then they're not really dead. They're still alive in your mind.' Death is shown to the reader as having a meaningful place. For *Redwall* is a portrait of a community, and the members of the community, the mice and other animals, learn to accept death as the story unfolds. Old Abbot Mortimer dies at the end of the book, and his death could be illustrative of the death of any beloved grandparent. '...I am not like the seasons. I cannot go on forever,' he says; and then, 'Life is good, my friends. I leave it to you. Do not be sad, for mine is a peaceful rest.' (pp.411 and 413)

Three very different novels: what do they share? I think they share sympathetic identification on the part of the authors with the protagonists, a commitment to good, interesting writing, and simple but powerful images.

There is plenty of realism in *Redwall*. There is also plenty of adventure, and plenty of humour. What seems very obvious as you read it is that the author is passionately involved in his own story. It is not just Matthias who you feel would die rather than allow Redwall to fall to Cluny and his horde, but the author as well. And so, odd though it may seem to an adult who is not used to children's fantasy, the reader believes passionately in the little mouse Matthias, in the courage and fortitude that lead him towards his destiny. It becomes credible – as all fantasy must, if it is to work.

After *Redwall* came *Mossflower*, and after *Mossflower* came *Mattimeo*, and then a second *Redwall* trilogy: *Mariel of Redwall*, *Salamandastron* and *Martin the Warrior*. At the time of writing, the second novel of the third trilogy has just been published. Here is an author who is enthusiastic about his created world! But *Redwall* was not envisaged as the first of a series with many sequels. It was accepted for publication and then the publishers suggested he should write more about the Abbey and its inhabitants, its friends and its enemies. The idea of writing more, said the author, appealed strongly. 'I wouldn't write about it if I didn't enjoy the imaginary world of Redwall. For me Redwall offers an escape – for four months of every year – from this world.'

In a way it is rather hard to imagine the first book, *Redwall*, existing on its own, because there are many untold stories suggested in it. There is the story of the past, the history of the Abbey and the role of Martin the Warrior who features in this first book talismanically and symbolically. It seems obvious that readers who enjoyed *Redwall* would want to know the story of Martin. But there is also the story of the future: what awaits Matthias, named by the dying Abbot as the Warrior Mouse of Redwall, with his sword Ratdeath? A sense of history is not just about the past but it is to do with an understanding, expressed in the story, of the way that as time moves on, things change. *Redwall* ends with Good triumphant (we are all very relieved about this!), but that does not mean that Evil has been wiped out forever. It is in this area too, in the up and down of Good and Evil, that fantasy is realistic. The struggle is a constant one, and if that can be exploited by fantasy writers who love their created worlds and want to go on writing about them, then I say, so much the better.

In fantasy, partly at least because of the form's tendency to run into sequels, the good versus evil axis is often left in the balance (maybe one could make a clever argument for fantasy being more realistic than 'realistic' fiction!). Good may have the upper hand at the end, but there is always the possibility that evil will recur. It would be a mistake to think that in children's literature good must triumph over evil at the end. Even when the narrative is not based on the good versus evil conflict, but on undergoing trials and overcoming adversity, a happy ending is not obligatory. Which is not to say that a scene like the end of *Hamlet* would go down well.

Children's literature nowadays allows for ambivalence. This is partly because the best children's writers do not moralise, so their stories do not end with an uplifting moral message, although nor, on the whole, do they end depressingly. At the end of *Black Unicorn*, for example, Tanaquil realises that the world she lives in is not a perfect world. She accepts that it is full of pain and cruelty and loss. So, being clever and tough, and with her faithful peeve beside her, she decides that she will try to change it for the better. *Redwall* ends with a death and an open future. *The Awesome Bird* ends with a delicate balance achieved.

It is also worth considering the rise of the interactive book and its influence on endings. Interactive books allow the reader to share the role of author. Interactive books for little ones have been around for years: flap books, pop-up books, books where things are hidden in the illustrations on each page so the child has to pore over the book to find them. But until quite recently publishers seemed to think that once a child had reached the age of seven or eight they should be reading books by starting at the beginning and carrying on through, word by word, to the end.

Not now. Along with children's TV programmes such as *Knightmare* (one child is in a fantasy world and able to act only on the instructions of a group of friends outside; each action has a particular outcome) and choice-centred computer games, there has been the publishing phenomenon of Steve Jackson and Ian Livingstone with their *Fighting Fantasy* Gamebooks. *The Warlock of Firetop Mountain* was the first of these *Fighting Fantasy* gamebooks, published in 1982. The series – approaching a hundred titles – has been a sensational success, with over 14 million copies sold and translated into 16 languages. These books set up a fantasy world full of potential dangers in which you, the reader, are the protagonist, and you wind your way through this world by making a series of choices. They are enormously popular with so-called reluctant readers, that is, children who find a whole continuous block of text too daunting, but for whom picture books are too babyish. The prose style of these books may be not much to write home about (the original ones in the series were written by Jackson and Livingstone, the later ones are 'presented' by them), and no characterisation is required, but they are written in very manageable paragraph-length chunks of text and they have to be – and obviously are – exciting and enthralling. The 'game' element is attractive to young readers, some of whom are not interested in a more conventional book. They can be read over and over again as different choices can be made, and thus different paths followed, each time. With the development of CD-Rom and increasingly sophisticated computer games, the chances are that inter-active written books may well also become more sophisti-cated. The connection between written text and computer image is here to stay. Already there are *Discworld* games (from the novels by Terry Pratchett) on CD-Rom, along with very effective fantasy games/worlds/stories such as *Myst*. Fantasy has come into its element with computers. Fantasy writers, and particularly those who want to write for children, should explore and exploit all the new possibilities that cyberspace opens up for them.

7
Dark fantasy: ghosts and other hauntings

Before we start on a discussion of ghost stories, or what is more commonly called dark fantasy, it may be most useful to ask yourself what it is that you, as a writer of these strange tales, are aiming to do. What response do you want, and hope, to get from your readers?

The response that you want to elicit is probably more specific than the responses you would hope to get to the kinds of fantasy that I have talked about so far. With the fantasy writing I have discussed so far you would want your readers to believe in the world you have created; you might perhaps want them to be entertained by, or enchanted with, or enamoured of your world; you might possibly, if your aim, for example, is to explore various manifestations of evil, want them to be enraged by it.

With ghost stories you either want to scare your readers or to unsettle them. Or indeed to scare or unsettle yourself. As in all fantasy, you want to take your readers on an exploration of another world. With dark fantasy the world you want to take them to is sinister, strange, not wholly explicable, and very possibly scary. And it exists alongside, or underneath, the familiar world.

The best, most effective ghost stories well up from within the everyday world.

You don't have to take your readers to a distant time or planet, or to a fantastical castle perched high on a magic mountain in a mythical landscape, or make your ghosts into vampires with pointy teeth and have blood dripping slowly down the castle walls.

If you do that, you increase your difficulties a hundred-fold, because you have to get your readers to believe first in your imagined world and then in the ghosts that inhabit it. You might well find that the energy and emotion that you should be using to create the sinister aspect of your story is being all used up in creating the fantasy world in which it happens.

If you want to scare or unsettle your readers most effectively, depict for them a world they recognise easily, one they are familiar with and have no difficulty in believing in, and then show them its nightmare side, its strange and sinister and scary underbelly. A great part of the sinister quality of ghost stories is in the connectedness they have with the ordinary world.

It is important then that the ordinary world should be easily credible. Remember, you are going to ask your readers to make a leap of faith into believing the inexplicable, the mysterious, possibly the supernatural. You will take your readers with you if you give them a firm base to stand on before making this leap.

In the previous chapter I talked about the importance of a realistically portrayed world, in relation to Brian Jacques' novel for younger readers, *Redwall*. The world of *Redwall* has a solidity that encourages the readers in their belief in the aspects that are not part of our 'normal' lives, that is, talking animals, mice who are monks, etc. The world in which the ghost story is set needs a similar, if not a greater, solidity. Why? Because you are going to ask of your readers that they believe in something, or that they see something, that probably they would rather not believe in. It is delightful, after all, to believe in talking mice, courageous badgers, etc., but it is perhaps not so delightful to be asked to believe in, say, the return of the dead. You must overcome your readers' resistance. One way is through the credibility of the world you describe, another is through the scepticism of one or more of your characters. Let us look at some examples.

Setting

Ramsey Campbell is one of the most respected and popular writers of ghost and horror stories currently at work. He has received the Bram Stoker Award, the World Fantasy Award three times and the British Fantasy Award seven times. He has lived on Merseyside all his life, and his work is imbued with a strong and specific sense of place. His stories are set in the late twentieth-century world of high-rise blocks, traffic jams and inner-city decay. He creates sinister tales out of seemingly mundane settings. 'The End of the Line' is the most recent story in his collection *Alone with the Horrors*, a collection that brings together in chronological order his stories over three decades, and is set in, of all unspooky places, a telesales office. The story is told almost entirely in dialogue: as the salesman goes through the alphabetical list of names he must ring, we realise that something is not right. There is something sinister about the 'P's. All around him salesmen and women are making their evening calls, creating ordinary evening annoyance for the householder at home. But the protagonist's conversations seem to slip constantly into a different gear ...

An earlier story, 'Mackintosh Willy' (1977), is set in the world of inner-city youth. I find this one a particularly unnerving story, and I'm not entirely sure why. Perhaps with the best stories one can never be quite certain why they work so well! The narrator is a young boy whose parents run a small newsagent's. He is a very ordinary kind of boy, with the ordinary amounts of boredom, bravado, timidity and attitude. He has always, in a very ordinary kind of way, been nervous of the hulking great tramp who lurks in the corner of the red-brick shelter by the boating pool in Newsham Park. The boy's experience is narrow: the small world of fair-grounds in the park in the summer, of pedestrian subways that only girls are wimpish enough to use, of policemen who automatically suspect lads of being up to no good, of boys struggling for status in a group, and of their first tentative fumblings with girls. It is a world of exhaust fumes, litter, broken glass and the tops of coca-cola bottles. And violence and retribution. The bottle tops are important: icons of twentieth-century ordinariness, used in this story for a foul purpose. Much more effective and sinister than a conventional tool of violence. Not that Ramsey Campbell spells out exactly what happens, or who does what to whom. As the boy who is telling the story says about the way the tramp got his name, from the names of three boys that had been written up in the shelter: MACK TOSH WILLY, which '... were partly erased, which no doubt was why one's mind tended to fill the gap.' (p.271)

Campbell wants his readers' minds to fill the gaps, just as in the telesales story the man hears – or mishears – what he wants or doesn't want to hear. In the telesales story the voices stumble and stutter and are uncertain. Fear lurks around us: at the end of the telephone line, in the red-brick shelter, behind the gleaming discarded bottle tops. It is not something that comes from elsewhere but comes from all around us, possibly even from inside us. 'Sometimes,' the boy thinks about Mackintosh Willy, 'I wonder how much of his monstrousness we created.' (p.268)

Ramsey Campbell writes of what he knows about: urban life in the late twentieth century, and reveals to his readers an aspect of it that they may not in the ordinary course of events be aware of. The credibility of the setting gives the readers a firm foundation from which they can peer into the abyss, and shudder.

Another respected writer of ghost, horror and dark fantasy is Lisa Tuttle. Many of her stories have as their protagonist an ordinary woman who lives in a recognisable contemporary world of work, lovers, partner or husband perhaps, children. Her story 'In Jealousy' appears in the anthology *Obsession* and is a ghost story of obsession and haunting of the living by the living. It takes place in three locales: China (a trip organised by the Society for Anglo-Chinese Understanding), London and Edinburgh. The narrator moves through a series of hotels, flats, wine bars and pubs. She is a woman adrift, floating through the world after the break-up of her marriage. She has an affair, she ends it. It is all familiar ground, a period of life experienced by countless women in the late twentieth century, women who are struggling to find their own way, who have not become caught up in domesticity, women who value their independence but also want and need to love and be loved.

Lisa Tuttle shows us the ghosts that haunt the most ordinary-seeming lives. She doesn't ask the reader to make a huge leap of the imagination into her narrator's life. The narrator's life is perfectly credible; and so the reader is more open to the ghosts that float up into it.

Suspense

As I hope I have shown, you don't need to go searching for an incredible scenario in which to present your unnerving vision. The world we live in will do fine. However, you don't want your readers to think that all they are being offered is a simple tale of growing up in Liverpool or of a failed relationship. You have something more interesting to show them than that, but you want to entwine them without giving it all away. In both the stories I have just talked about the authors use a very simple device. They tell the reader right at the beginning that something weird is going to happen. The boy in 'Mackintosh Willy' wonders, as we have heard, whether the tramp's monstrousness was at least partially created by the boys themselves. End of the first paragraph: 'Wondering helps me not to ponder my responsibility for what happened at the end.' (p.268) Responsibility for what? The end of what? It would be a dull (or maybe very nervous!) reader who didn't want to find out the answer to those two questions.

'In Jealousy' starts: 'I've always liked ghost stories without believing in them. But this one I believe, because it happened to me.' (p.88) The device of the true story: you can't believe that this woman would lie!

Of course, simply to say at the beginning of your story that something weird is going to unfold isn't enough: the suspense must be built up throughout the story.

One way of building up the suspense is for your protagonist to become increasingly unnerved, because increasingly aware that something out of the ordinary is going on. Very often the protagonist of a ghost story starts off as an un-believer, a sceptic in all matters ghostly and supernatural. In Lisa Tuttle's story 'In Jealousy' the first-person narrator has always been sceptical about ghosts, until the very events of this story occur. The assumption (or device) here is that the reader, too, is sceptical.The author is allowing the reader to say: 'Ghosts? Pah! What nonsense!'. In fact the author is encouraging the reader to say that, just as the protagonist of the story does. The author appears to be sympathising with the reader, appearing to expect scepticism from her. But then ... the strangeness begins, the protagonist becomes just a little less certain of the cut-and-dried stable foundation of the universe, and as the protagonist becomes unsettled, so too does the reader.

A classic example of the sceptical protagonist is Professor Parkins in a story by an undoubted master of the form, M.R. James, 'Oh, Whistle, and I'll Come to You, My Lad'. M.R. James remains hugely influential on contemporary writers. Ramsay Campbell says that he learned first from the tales of M.R. James that 'the best work achieves its effects through the use of style, the selection of language.' (Introduction to *Alone with the Horrors*). Lisa Tuttle remembers how as a child she would take down from her father's bookshelves fat anthologies with titles like 'A Hundred Strange and Fantastic Tales' or 'A Century of Ghost Stories', and lose herself in tales by classic masters of the genre such as M.R. James, Arthur Machen, Ambrose Bierce and Oliver Onions. When grown up and starting out on her own writing career she found an old secondhand copy of M.R. James's Collected Works. All the stories were wonderful, and to this day, she says, he 'remains terrific'. So, if you want to write ghost stories, you couldn't do better than take out a volume of M.R. James and see how he manages it.

Professor Parkins is such a sceptic that he is even able, at the beginning of the story, to speculate in a completely abstract way about what would be the case if the figure following him along the seashore were the devil. As we have just seen Professor Parkins finding something on an ancient mystical site, slipping it into his pocket and walking off with it, we, the readers, cannot help but feel that maybe he is being a bit cavalier with his speculations. However sceptical we may be, our scepticism must pale before someone who can think casually, dismissively, about being followed by the devil when in his pocket he carries something that he knows, and we know, comes from a time when things were different and the devil lurked close by ... We, the readers, cannot help but know better than Professor Parkins. We suspect his vaunted scepticism may turn out to be highly dangerous. 'Watch out!' we want to cry. 'Chuck it away before it is too late!' However sceptical we may have been before the story began, we cannot help now but fear the worst.

And the threat, the uncertainty, is still no more than a distant figure along the beach!

We must read on.

As well as illustrating the importance of setting and the role of the sceptical protagonist, 'Oh, Whistle' offers an example of another common ingredient of a ghost story: the bargain. In this instance the Professor doesn't know that he has entered into a bargain with the Devil, but we do. The words: 'Oh, whistle, and I'll come to you, my lad', make up a sinister promise. The story shows the fulfillment of that promise. Part of what keeps us reading is the desire to know precisely how that promise will be fulfilled. Readers are naturally curious creatures: by exploiting that curiosity you are creating suspense.

Scariness

What is the scariest part of 'Oh, Whistle, and I'll Come to You, My Lad'? Is it not the bed that is meant to be empty, the sheets that have not been used and yet are crumpled and twisted? The maid comes in with a blanket, 'Which bed should I put it on, sir?' she asked.' (p.137) It is at once obvious to her, and to us, that both beds have been slept in. How can the Professor bear to spend another night in the room?

Again, it is the ordinary that is imbued with dread. The spare bed in a room in a little seaside inn is the site for something fearful and horrible.

How do you know that something is going to scare your readers? Of course you can't be absolutely certain, but you can be pretty sure that anything *you* don't find scary, *they* won't find scary. As with any kind of writing, if you approach it by thinking along the lines of 'what will sell well?', or 'what hasn't been done yet?' then what you write will lack conviction and so it will automatically lack power. This is not to say that there are not some mediocre writers who sell well, but one must generously assume that they did not set out to be mediocre. In dark fantasy this affects whatever it is that is meant to be scary. You may think, 'Skulls and eyesockets are old hat, but what about a dear departed one's teeth as the central image for a tale of haunting?' But if *you* don't find them troubling, then no-one else will. There are however writers who have been terrified of teeth (and there are probably many learned psychoanalytic papers to be written on them): read Edgar Allan Poe's 'Berenice', for example, for a really toothily troubling tale. And just floated up from my unconscious is the memory of a strangely unsettling story by Lisa Tuttle featuring horses' teeth.

Lisa Tuttle puts it like this: 'When I was young I used to spend a lot of time telling stories to my friends and when I tried to think of a story to tell them I would think of something that scared me.' She describes finishing one of her earlier novels, *Familiar Spirit*, late one night when she was alone in a house. It is certainly a novel that I wouldn't want to read late at night while alone in a house, particularly as it is about a woman alone (or so she thinks) in a house ... (I had to stop reading her novel *Gabriel* while I was pregnant: it is about a haunting that culminates in a birth!) She learned her lesson, and now knows that there are 'things I wouldn't want to be writing too late at night.'

So if you find yourself at your writing desk at midnight in an empty house, with the wind sobbing round the gables, and the floorboards in the corridor outside your room creaking and groaning, and suddenly your window flies open and a gust of rain spatters your desk, and you say, 'Oh drat, it seems to be raining,' and you get up to shut the window without even bothering to check for disembodied hands on the windowsill, and then sit down, yawning, to finish your paragraph ... Chances are your readers won't be frightened either.

Gwyneth Jones, who sometimes uses the name Ann Halam when she is writing for younger readers, and whose dark fantasies for younger readers include *King Death's Garden*, *The Fear Man*, and *The Haunting of Jessica Raven*, echoes the sentiments of Lisa Tuttle: 'When I am writing,' she says, 'I expect the hairs to stand up on the back of my neck.'

Lisa Tuttle again: 'The most effective writing aims for the universal, but it cannot be universal if it is not also deeply personal.' She makes an interesting comparison between writing ghost stories and writing about sex, for it requires 'a huge amount of bravery or indifference to put down your innermost fears on the page for other people to read – and to judge.'

Ghost stories for children

There are many excellent ghost stories for children. A hundred or so years ago, when ghost stories were enormously popular, they were not considered inappropriate for children, just as the subject of death itself was not considered inappropriate. The two, of course, go together. Think of Charles Dickens' *A Christmas Carol*, for example, or Charles Kingsley's *The Water Babies* (a ghost story at least insofar as it portrays life after death).

But more recently dark fantasies, deaths and hauntings have in some circles been deemed unsuitable. Children's writing is perhaps more a victim of fashion than other forms of literature. This is probably because some people are attracted by the authoritarian opportunities it offers for saying what children ought, or ought not, to be reading. These people should be ignored. (The old vexed question of a canon of great literature has recently surfaced in relation to children's books with the introduction of the national curriculum and recommended texts for schools.)

Look instead at the dark fantasy and ghost stories by good writers such as Joan Aiken, Gwyneth Jones, Penelope Lively, Philippa Pearce and Terry Pratchett, to mention only some of them. Look at the anthologies compiled by Aidan Chambers I mentioned before.

Gwyneth Jones has written about the question:

> Children know about the bad things, they are perhaps more afraid of them than we realise. While I don't want to compete with reality, and am always conscious of not wanting to invade reality's territory, I do deal in my fiction with seriously horrible things. It may be that I am offering a kind of fairground ride, something that is exciting and sensational, but children know about the bad things already, they recognise what it is we're talking about.

You will find that to write ghost stories for younger readers is not so very different from writing for adults, although you will have to be even more than usually alert to the everyday manifestations of contemporary life. M.R. James remains as good a model as any. Let's look at Ann Halam's *King Death's Garden*. The protagonist, twelve year old Maurice, is another sceptic like Professor Parkins. He, and the reader, can sneer at the gullibility of the batty old scientist who left his house to his housekeeper, Maurice's great aunt Ada, with whom Maurice now lives. The old fellow believed there were fairies at the bottom of his garden. Like Maurice, we, readers in the contemporary world, know all about those fake fairy photographs, don't we? It is all part and parcel of Lewis Carroll and other Edwardian gentlemen with big moustaches who had a special fondness for little wispily-clad girls of nine and ten.

But soon the reader and the protagonist begin to part company, for it becomes increasingly obvious to the reader that maybe the old fellow wasn't such a batty old fool as we thought. As Maurice spends more and more time in King Death's Garden – the cemetery over the wall at the bottom of the garden – he is becoming, unwittingly, more and more enmeshed in the land of the dead. We begin to suspect that he will not be able just to leave it when he wants. In the Garden he visits worlds and times not his own. And such a privilege – if it is a privilege, for such visits are not altogether pleasant – must be paid for.

Maurice has made a deal with Death and he doesn't even know he's made it. But we do.

What form will the payment take? What are the demands of Death/the Devil/the darkness? Will the protagonist escape in time, and if so, how will he manage it? These are the same questions that captured the reader's interest in the M.R. James story, 'Oh, Whistle ...'

And meanwhile the author is building up a detailed picture of the contemporary world through the stories of other characters: at school there is Jasmin Kapoor, who is different from the other children and is not allowed to mix with them, but is picked up by a big black car every day; there is Mary the home help who is secretly a sculptor; and there is great aunt Ada herself with her own secret, which is buried in King Death's Garden. This is the living, breathing, complex contemporary world on which Maurice, asthmatic, self-indulgent Maurice has turned his back.

And then Maurice's companions from the Garden come to get him. He has ignored all warnings, and now he hears foot-steps on the stairs, whisperings outside his room at night. One evening he is on his way home from school:

> The bus was very crowded. Figures pressed together in the aisle: wet umbrellas, shopping bags, solemn faces – Maurice turned round again quickly. He didn't want to count the standing travellers. He had an uneasy feeling it would come to more than the bus company allowed. (*King Death's Garden* p.95)

You don't need a one-eyed, foul-breathed monster with a rusty knife, or an indescribable something (covered in slime), to conjure up terrors in the human heart. Some crumpled sheets, a crowded bus: these are the kinds of things you see out of the corner of your eye. It is their very ordinariness that makes them so sinister. These are the kinds of things that well up from the innermost recesses of the mind, the unconscious if you like, or that part of the imagination that is not sunny and creative, and take you by surprise. This is dark fantasy: the shadow side of the human soul.

In all the stories mentioned in this chapter the protagonist has come to believe in the existence of a shadowland. If you, as a writer, concentrate on opening up your protagonist's mind to the shadowland, then your readers will allow their minds to be opened too. Your task is to scare and unsettle your readers. First, you must scare and unsettle yourself, and the protagonist of your story. And remember, if you want to keep your readers scared, they mustn't be allowed to shut that shadowland out. So don't place it far away. The world of ghosts and hauntings lurks very close by this world, just a blink, or a word, or a glance away.

8
Comic fantasy

It is probably true to say that the funniest kind of comedy seems to flow naturally on the page. It is also probably true to say that almost undoubtedly the natural comic flow has been worked and reworked and then reworked again. When you read something that makes you laugh, the chances are that the author did not sit down, and, amidst gales of solitary laughter, type out hysterical scene after hysterical scene. Hard graft is required to make things seem natural.

Which is just to say that writing comic fantasy is no easier than writing any other kind of fantasy, and may, indeed, even be harder.

One of the difficulties is that very few things are objectively funny. Finding something funny is notoriously subjective, and what may have you rolling on the floor, gasping for breath, with tears streaming down your face, may leave another person with a look of polite bewilderment on theirs. I can think of various examples: I remember demanding, incoherent with laughter, that a friend of mine read Beachcomber's 'Trousers Over Africa', and waiting for the first peal of laughter, and waiting, and waiting; and finally retrieving the book, saying rather defensively, 'Well, I think it's funny.'

Terry Pratchett tries his comic novels out on as many people as possible while they are still in draft form. In an interview conducted by Paul Kincaid he said: 'There is no such thing as a bad comment, because if (a friend) doesn't think a joke is funny when I did then there's something wrong with that joke, I've got to look hard at it and think: is it because a lot of people will get it and a lot of people won't? – fair enough, there are lots of other jokes on that page so it doesn't matter. Or have I slipped up on something that I thought was funny and the rest of the world doesn't?'

He goes on to give an example of the hard graft behind spontaneous-seeming comedy:

> ... It was a big eye-opener for me that in the Marx brothers films, which always give the appearance of absolute spontaneity, the gags were tried and retried and honed. They used to take the earlier films out on the road as vaudeville acts and guys would sit there with notebooks and time the laughs. And every day they would hone and cut and put new things in. What they ended up with was something that sounded totally spontaneous, but people had sweated blood for a couple of months getting that spontaneity exactly right. And I actually approve of that idea. There is nothing wrong with testing your sense of humour repeatedly against other people. (*Interzone* 25, Sept–Oct 1988)

But you have to start somewhere. Your starting point must be something that you, the writer, find funny. It is no good trying to please other people and not yourself. You cannot approach your writing by thinking, 'People always laugh at fat men slipping on banana skins, so I'll put a fat man slipping on a banana skin into my story, even although I myself (fat, thin or middlesized) don't find it very funny.' It is unlikely that you would be able to write it in such a way that it appeared funny. And remember, writing is all! The most unpromising material can be transformed by your writing of it.

Start off in good faith with an idea or a character that you yourself find extremely comic. Now this is where a writing group could be very useful. You laughed when you read it out to yourself, you laughed again when you read it out to your dog, and you laughed when you read it out to your writers' group. The last case is the telling one. Did anyone laugh with you?

Characters, or events, are not in themselves necessarily funny. It is all a question – the all-important question – of how you tell them. You can elicit laughter through surprise, overturning expectations, paradoxes, impossibilities, deliberate anachronisms, exaggeration, absurdity ...

And perhaps most importantly of all, through sympathy. If you want to sustain a comic fantasy, it is essential that you feel sympathy for your characters and for your chosen genre, for fantasy itself.

Although this may sound odd, it is necessary to take something seriously before you can glean comic riches from it.

Characters

If you flick through any comic fantasy titles, for adults or
children, the chances are that you will find protagonists who
are likeable types but are looked down on for one reason or
another. They may well appear to be ineffectual, or
unsuccessful, or awkward, or misfits of some kind. It is very
unlikely that you will find a protagonist of a comic fantasy
who starts off enormously rich, or handsome (unless he's also
very stupid: handsome but stupid is OK for a comic fantasy
protagonist, as long as he is sweet-tempered as well), or
successful, or surrounded with admirers or lovers. The
protagonist may well wish to be enormously rich, etc.: the
comedy will arise then from the gap between their desires or
expectations (high) and the reality of their position (low), and
might be sustained by their attempts to get from one to the
other, the latter to the former.

Robert Rankin, author of high-selling comic fantasies, such
as the 'now legendary' (as it says on the cover) *Brentford
Trilogy, The Greatest Show Off Earth, Raiders of the Lost Car Park*
and others said: 'All my books have a formula – an individual
being put upon by a large organisation in one form or another
– which is basically my plan of life.' (*Writing Magazine*,
October 1994)

With other writers it is not necessarily a 'large organisation'
that does the putting upon, it may be a group of individuals,
or even one individual, but as like as not they will be
representatives of, if not a specific organisation, then an
abstract Authority, probably in a rigidly authoritarian form.

Think of menopausal Diana in Jane Palmer's *The Planet
Dweller*. The Authority she first comes up against appears in
the form of Dr Spalding, who ignores her demands for HRT
and insists on prescribing tranquillizers for her hot flushes
instead.

Think of Rincewind, a wizard on Terry Pratchett's
Discworld, who after sixteen years of study has failed even to
achieve level one of wizardry, and is even thought to be
incapable of achieving level zero, which most normal people
are born at. You can tell he's a wizard because his pointy hat
has 'Wizzard' badly embroidered on it. What's more, he 'has
the scrubby kind of beard that looks like the kind of beard
worn by people who weren't cut out by nature to be beard
wearers.' (*Sourcery*, p.17)

Think of Mildred Hubble in Jill Murphy's *The Worst Witch* books, with her baggy socks and rickety broomstick, the only girl in the school to end up with a tabby rather than a black cat, sneered at by the goody-goodies and constantly picked upon by the horrible Miss Hardbroom.

Think of Robert Rankin's Jim Pooley and John Omally, chronically unemployed and chronically thirsty, propping up the bar in the Flying Swan.

All of these are no-hopers in terms of conventional expectations.

Think of the human race in Douglas Adams' *The Hitch Hiker's Guide to the Galaxy*: on the verge of extinction as the book opens. No hope at all, and as for its sole surviving representative ...

Or take one step up the ladder from humankind, and think of all the gods of the world, all immortal but alas not blessed with eternal youth, now crotchety and decrepit in the Sunnyvoyde Residential Home for retired deities in Tom Holt's *Odds and Gods*. The authority figure there? Mrs Henderson the terrifying matron before whom all gods tremble.

Plot

Comic characters like these give you your story. Comedy is anti-authoritarian, it is about overturning hierarchies and messing around with the status quo. Your plot can consist of following these characters through a series of adventures to see how they escape from the authority that oppresses them. This is the libertarian aspect of comedy, the escape from constraints. It can also consist of following your characters through a series of adventures that will reveal to themselves, and to others, their true worth. This is the romance aspect of comedy, the quest for the true self.

Comic stories and novels require a basic plot, however much you may like to embellish it with preposterous events, strange coincidences, sudden strokes of fate, or, as Terry Pratchett does so well, series of chronic mismatches between destiny and desire. Indeed perhaps it is an indication of Pratchett's skill that he even manages to create delightful comedy from a character who is *not* out-of-place, misunderstood, overlooked, etc., but is very happy in his job and has no desire or pretensions to do anything else. I'm referring here to the Librarian of the Unseen University. Although perhaps it is something to do with his being an orang-utan.

If you don't have a basic plot, then you will find you are writing a series of gags, which is fine for a stand-up comic, but does not sustain a book or story. It is worth thinking of a TV series like *Red Dwarf*: full of gags, but each episode, only half an hour long, has a story, however preposterous that story may be. Which is not to say that gags are not important. You want your readers to be laughing at every page.

The story may be as simple as: characters who might expect to be on the margins – of life, society and the story – for example, blokes who spend their time propping up bars, middle-aged women who are considered to be a bit batty – find themselves suddenly, reluctantly perhaps, playing the role of hero or heroine or central character in their own stories.

Surprise

Comic writing needs to be constantly surprising. If it is predictable, then you will elicit a groan rather than a laugh when you reach your punchline. But you don't need elaborate surprises. Simple dialogue, in which you allow characters to speak in unpredictable ways, can be very effective. Here is a snatch of dialogue from Terry Pratchett's *Sourcery:*

> THERE IS NO HOPE FOR THE FUTURE, said Death.
> 'What does it contain, then?'
> ME.
> 'Besides you I mean!'
> Death gave him a puzzled look. I'M SORRY?
> The storm reached its howling peak overhead. A seagull went past backwards.
> 'I meant,' said Ipslore, bitterly, 'what is there in this world that makes living worth while?'
> Death thought about it.
> CATS, he said eventually, CATS ARE NICE.(p.11)

The reader's expectations (and Ipslore's expectations) are overturned in the mismatch of seriousness and triviality in Death's response. And the 'eventually' is perfect. Pratchett is fond of the delayed response in dialogue. Here he is, in the same interview as quoted above, describing how *Wyrd Sisters* began for him: ' ... with *Wyrd Sisters* I had the image of the blasted heath, the storm, the three figures over the cauldron, the eldritch screech of "When shall we three meet again?" and then there's a long pause before someone says, "Well, I can't make Tuesday."'

The expectations of the genre are mocked: the tragic portentousness of Shakespeare's three witches undermined for the rest of the book by those five words; the central fantasy figure of a once powerful wizard, on a cliff edge in a howling storm what's more, trounced in the most unlikely way by Death ... And yet the mockery is affectionate. Indeed, Death has proved to be one of Pratchett's most likeable and popular characters.

Death's capital letters when he speaks are a running joke throughout the Discworld novels, and Terry Pratchett makes other typographical jokes. The enormously tall adopted dwarf Carrot, for example, is very good at the misplaced comma. On the whole however I would be wary of mis-spellings and mispronunciations as a source of jokes. I am surprised by the number of writers of books for children who make their characters hopeless at spelling. As often as not the child reader will not notice that the word is misspelt, or if they do they think it a mistake. And, in general, mistakes in speech and writing can be interpreted as an invitation to laugh at rather than with a character, to laugh, that is, at their stupidity. Stupid characters do not make good comedy, although there is plenty of comic mileage to be got from ones who are thought by everyone around them to be stupid ...

If you are determined to write comic novels and stories, then you couldn't do better than to choose comic fantasy as your favoured mode. Not that it is necessarily easier to make comedy out of fantasy, rather than, for example, out of main-stream social drama. But it helps that fantasy offers such enor-mous scope. Fantasy offers magic, philosophy, adventure, derring-do, romance, and all the deeply serious matters that I have been talking about throughout this book. And there is nothing like having deeply serious matters, whether it is the end of the world, the coming of the Antichrist, or the ongoing, if niggling question of what actually is the meaning of life, to underpin your comedy.

In Tom Holt's *Odds and Gods*, for example, the question of what it means to be a god runs throughout the book. Osiris, on the run from his lawyer godson who wants to certify him insane, is holed up in Wolverhampton at Sandra's mum's house. When Sandra tells him that the good people of

Wolverhampton have a tendency towards disbelief, Osiris knows at once why he is feeling so weak. We then have an exposition of the relationship between gods and their believers, and the relationship between the manifestation of a god and the nature of the belief in him, that would not sit amiss on a first year philosophy course, except that the absurdity of the example given makes it comic:

> ... Belief is to gods what atmosphere is to other, rather more temporary life-forms; they live in it, and it shapes them, in the way that millions of tons of water overhead shape the curiously designed fish that live at the very bottom of the sea. This can, of course, have its unfortunate side. When, for example, the Quizquacs of central Peru had finally had enough of their god Tlatelolco's obsession with human sacrifice *à la nouvelle cuisine* (one small human heart, garnished with fine herbs and served with the blood *under* the meat) they exacted a terrible revenge, not by ceasing to believe in him, but by believing in him with a fervour never before encountered in such a pathologically devout race as the Quizquacs. They also chose to believe in him in his aspect as an excessively timid field vole inhabiting an enclosed kitchen full of hungry cats. (*Odds and Gods*, p.53)

In the example quoted above, nouvelle cuisine becomes a part of a human sacrifice cult. In Terry Pratchett's *Men at Arms*, political correctness has dictated how the men-at-arms of the title, the City Guard (Night Watch) of the city of Ankh-Morpork, shall be made up: from ethnic minorites (one dwarf and one troll) and the obligatory woman (she is not in fact just, or only, a woman, which adds further comic mayhem to the plot). Nouvelle cuisine and political correctness are both vagaries, or excrescences (depending on how you look at these things) of contemporary life.

Comedy is a touchstone of social change. A lot of contemporary comic fantasy is absolutely reliant on the sharp-eyed observation of mores, customs and attitudes from the world we inhabit. It is by transferring those observations to the invented fantasy world that the comedy is generated.

In neither of the above examples are the characters themselves being sneered at. Tom Holt's Osiris (whose parts are never put together in quite the right order by his shortsighted sister/wife Isis), and Terry Pratchett's Cuddy the dwarf, Detritus the troll and Angua the woman (or so everyone thinks) elicit the readers' sympathies. What is held up for our mockery is the dimwitted ideological reasoning that has an ethnic minority policy and no sense of the humanity of the people involved; or a lack of imagination (in Wolverhampton, perhaps unfairly) that allows for nothing outside a dreary materialism of on-the-dot mealtimes and dust-free furniture. What is held up for our censure – to a greater or lesser extent in all the books mentioned in this chapter – is oppression, discrimination and exploitation.

Comic fantasy, it seems to me, is a deeply moral genre. This is partly, at least, because it looks clear-eyed at the world around us. Which may seem paradoxical, but isn't really. Here's Terry Pratchett again on the value of opening the doors of his fiction to aspects of the real world:

> You have to have a serious skeleton to the book, and I don't just mean Death. But you need balance, too. I've read too many fantasy writers who are too keen on unicorns or listening to the elves singing, or who go the other way for unrelieved humour that is completely gag-driven from first to last.
>
> Fantasy doesn't have to be fantastic. American writers in particular find this harder to grasp. You need to have your feet on the ground as much as your head in the clouds. The cute dragon that sits on your shoulder also craps all down your back, but this makes it more interesting because it gives it an added dimension. Similarly, the fact that Ankh-Morpork is knee-deep in slurry half the time doesn't make it any less a fantasy city. (interviewed by Brendan Wignall, MILLION 5/Interzone 51 (joint issue) Sept–Oct 1991, revised by Terry Pratchett, 1996)

Comedy is produced through outrageous juxtapositions and extraordinary links being formed, or forced, between disparate ideas. And all done with speed, inner logic and, to quote from what might be described as a comic nightmare, Jonathan Coe's Oh, What a Carve Up! , 'the necessary brio' (notwithstanding my warning above, this is a phrase around which Coe builds an excellent (mis)spelling joke).

There is nothing simple about things that are funny. (Freud wrote a whole book about it: Jokes and their Relation to the Unconscious, so it must be deadly serious.)

Perhaps I had better quote here Interzone magazine's stern fantasy critic, Chris Gilmore:

> Humorous fantasy depends on one or both of two ingredients: the deployment of perverse ingenuity within the discipline of

the chosen mode (usually sword and sorcery), and mismatch between manner and matter.

He goes on to say, even more sternly:

> The first requires original talent, and cannot be taught; the second is a skill which can be learnt, but runs the risk of becoming no less stylized than its target. (October 1995)

So, polish up your ingenuity, keep your mind loose, not stuck in a rut (this is the danger of stylisation), and take a leap of faith.

To end the chapter I will quote Robert Rankin again as he makes it sound much easier than Chris Gilmore does, but as you will see, there is a catch ... for someone else!

'The best stuff,' says Robert Rankin, 'is straight on to the page and then straight on to the typewriter because it has come straight out of your head and it is right.'

The interviewer then comments that that must be why Rankin's work is 'so fresh and spontaneous,' and Rankin replies: 'The laboured stuff is crossed out because I know that I am doing it. I know that if I have been working on one paragraph and I have written it three times, it goes in the bin. Unless it comes straight out, it is wrong, it is awkward, it does not fit.' (*Writing Magazine*, October 1994)

This contradicts what Terry Pratchett said about the Marx brothers and the need constantly to test your sense of humour against other people, and seems to suggest that I was completely wrong in my opening remarks to this chapter. All writers work differently, and there is no absolute best way, but the spontaneity of Robert Rankin's writing is not quite as spontaneous as he first suggests. The interviewer's next question is extremely revealing: 'Are your books heavily edited?' she asks.

And the answer is definitely yes.

Robert Rankin has an editor, it seems, who works and reworks.

Which brings us to the subject of the next chapter, in which I will consider what happens beyond the confines of your solitary room, when you and your manuscript head out into the unknown, dangerous terrain of ... the world of publishing.

9
From draft to proof

Beginning writers of fantasy – and of its sister genre, science fiction – are at quite an advantage in having a network of groups of fans and writers scattered around the country, in having a stream of self-published fanzines available to send work to and for seeing what other writers are up to; and in having a series of local, national and indeed international conventions, where they can meet readers, editors, illustrators and other writers, published, self-published or as yet unpublished. In other words, there is a community of fantasy writers and readers, and a mingling and crossover of people who are professionally and non-professionally involved.

Any aspirant fantasy writer would be well advised to join the BSFA (British Science Fiction Association) as a first step. It might also be worth joining the BFS (Brititsh Fantasy Society), especially if you are interested in dark fantasy and horror. The BSFA publishes a bi-monthly magazine called *Vector*, which has feature articles and book reviews on science fiction and fantasy, a newsletter – a bit like a public noticeboard – with news of conventions, meetings, publications, films, internet newsgroups and general gossip about what's going on, and, twice a year, *Focus*, a magazine by and for professional, amateur and simply enthusiastic writers of science fiction and fantasy. The BFS also publishes a regular newsletter and a variety of magazines and pamphlets containing fiction, reviews, interviews, etc.

I would then recommend that you send stories to fanzines and other amateur magazines. That is the first step in going public. You, and others, can then look at your work objectively now that you are no longer hugging it to your chest.

Going professional

In this chapter I am going to go through the various processes awaiting the writer once she, or he, has reached the final page, has typed 'ends' and has run a word count. If you haven't done a word count, do so now. Wherever you are planning to send your work, the potential publisher will want to know how long it is. You too should know before you send your work in to anyone what are the sorts of lengths that that publisher normally publishes. If somebody is looking for stories of no more than 5000 words for a fantasy anthology, then there is no point sending in your unutterably brilliant 10,000 word story of magic, myth and mystery. Indeed, not only is there no point but it could be detrimental. If an editor has turned down your first sub-mission because it is twice as long as the stated length, then she is likely to be prejudiced, however subliminally or unconsciously, against your next submission, even if it fulfils all the stated criteria. And with reason: you will already have wasted her time by drawing her attention to something that is unsuitable, and you will have shown yourself to be unconcerned with matters of detail, not a good sign in any writer, least of all perhaps in a fantasy writer who is in the business of creating credible worlds.

The first step, then, to getting your work accepted for professional publication is to submit it. There are different processes according to whether you are writing short fiction or novels, so I will deal with them separately. But first, some important rules, which may seem obvious but which bear repeating: any manuscript should be typed on one side of the sheet only, in double spacing, with wide margins, each page numbered and with a running head. The running head can be the title, part of the title (recommended if your title is longer than three words), or part of the title and your last name.

What do you want to achieve? You want to achieve some-thing that is easy to read, that requires no more effort on the part of the editor to whom you are submitting it than that she turns over each sheet and reads on to the next. Do not staple your manuscript together; put it looseleaf, but neatly, into a folder.

Always send a stamped address envelope (with correct postage) for the return of your manuscript.

Competitions

There is a large number of competitions for unpublished short stories. Unless the genre or subject matter is specified otherwise, there is no reason why you should not submit fantasy. Many national and local newspapers and magazines (and especially women's magazines) run regular writing competitions, as do regional arts associations and organisations. The judges for children's stories (for example the *Independent*/Scholastic Books have an annual competition, details of which appear every Spring in the *Independent on Saturday*) would probably be very surprised if many of the entries were not fantasy based.

I cannot stress enough the value of entering competitions. The psychological benefit comes from having some of your work out there, in the public domain, being read by strangers who will be reading it as work standing on its own, not work written by nice old so-and-so who has been in the writing group for four years. When other work is rejected, or you fail to get placed in a competition, then the optimism necessary to writers (the optimistic belief that you will finish the novel, that you will get it published, that somehow it is all worthwhile and that what you have written is not rubbish or a collection of crazy ideas) is upheld by the knowledge that someone, somewhere, is reading, and taking seriously, your work. The simple discipline of providing a nice clean copy and sending it off with the appropriately filled-in entry form is also psychologically beneficial. It makes you feel that you are part of a community of writers.

And, of course, most important of all, you might win a prize. You're certainly not going to win a prize if you don't enter. The prize will consist of money perhaps – and there is little more encouraging to a new writer than having their work paid for – publication if you win first prize, and seeing your name in print even if the story isn't published. This last is not only gratifying but is the first step in getting your name known.

Short stories and the magazine market

You are now going to submit a story to a magazine for commercial publication. You will already have had one or two pieces in a fanzine, and you may perhaps have won third prize in a national short story competition (for example, the biennial *Stand* competition, or the annual Bridford Arts). You will decide which magazine you are going to submit your story to, whether it's going to be a genre magazine like *Interzone*, whether it's going to be a small literary magazine like *Stand* or, if you think your story would have particular appeal to a female readership, one of the women's magazines. Check the criteria first. *Writers' and Artists' Yearbook* provides a list of magazines with their criteria for submissions, but you should anyway be familiar with any magazine to which you are submitting work. There is no point in submitting a story to a magazine that does not accept unsolicited manuscripts. Most magazines state their policy somewhere on the title page amongst the details on subscriptions and letters to the editor. *Interzone*, for example, states: 'Stories, in the 2000 to 6000 word range, should be sent singly and each one must be accompanied by a stamped self-addressed envelope of adequate size.' Do not send your story if it is the wrong length, however brilliant you think it is. Either send another story, or rework it to make it the right length. Do not, if it is 500 words too long, print it out in smaller point size and hope the editor won't notice the length. She will.

Other outlets for short stories are provided by anthologies. Keep an eye on the letters columns and small ads in the appropriate magazines to see if anyone is putting together an anthology of previously unpublished short fiction. Again, you don't need to restrict yourself to genre magazines, but keep an eye on publications like the *London Review of Books* or *The Times Literary Supplement*.

I thought it might be worth looking at the copyright page of *The Penguin Book of Modern Fantasy by Women* (published 1995) to see where the stories had first been published. Of the stories first published within the last ten years, they first appeared in *Omni* magazine, *Firebird*, *Isaac Asimov's Science Fiction Magazine*, the *Magazine of Fantasy and Science Fiction*, the *New Yorker*, and a variety of anthologies, such as *Skin of the Soul*, ed. Lisa Tuttle, *Despatches from the Frontiers of the Female Mind*, ed. Jen Green and Sarah LeFanu, and *The Thirteenth Ghost Book*, ed. James Hale. The majority of the magazines are American. There is no reason why you should not submit to American magazines from Britain – and vice versa of course. In genre writing, and for historical reasons particularly with fantasy and science fiction, there is a great deal of exchange between the UK and the USA. And in terms of genre magazines, there is more scope in the USA than in the UK, which is why a British publication like *The Penguin Book of Modern Fantasy by Women* includes so many stories first published in America.

With your manuscript you will send, of course, an s.a.e (a stamped addressed envelope, big enough to fit the manuscript into) and a covering letter. Do not spend days composing a covering letter, but be practical. All that needs to go into a covering letter is what it is that you are enclosing. Describe your story in one sentence without making any value judgments. In my experience as an editor both of short and long fiction there is something very offputting about being told what to think of something before you have even read it. Do not put: 'This is a deeply moving story set on the wonderfully realised world of Brilliancia', or 'I am sure you will enjoy this witty intelligent tale of urban terrorism in the late twenty-first century'. It is up to the editor to decide whether your story is deeply moving or witty and intelligent: do not preempt her.

But do not be shy. Do include in your covering letter the details of any prizes you have won or indeed been shortlisted for. This is not blowing your own trumpet. Rather, it is showing that you are a serious writer whose work has been looked at, and responded to favourably, by other professionals in the field.

Novels

Submit your novel only to the appropriate publishing houses and save yourself a lot of heartache. With novels, the same rules regarding return postage, covering letter, etc. apply as for short stories. In order to find the right publishing house you should first familiarise yourself with who publishes what. However much you are part of the world of fantasy writing you may not know the exact details of who publishes which books. Go into a big local bookshop with pencil and paper and do some research. Find out, by looking in the copyright pages of the books, who was the original, the first, publisher of all the books that you like and admire and that you think are similar in content, or form, or style, to the novel you have just finished. The copyright page is usually the second or fourth page into the book, on a verso page, which means the left-hand page. If you look at the front of this book you will see 'First published 1996' and then the name and address of the publishing house. You need to find the original publisher because there is no point in sending your manuscript to a paperback publisher if they do not publish original paperbacks, that is, if they only publish in paperback books that have already appeared in hardback. Nowadays, as a result of the mergers that have taken place in the publishing industry throughout the 1980s and 1990s, many companies have their own hardback and paperback imprints (in the old days paperback houses used to buy from hardback houses). So vast are these companies that it is essential that you send your manuscript to the right imprint. It is no longer a question of a couple of editors on the first floor passing manuscripts to each other.

Let us say, for example, that you have just finished a novel that you think is suitable for the young adult market, and that is not, you feel, unlike Tanith Lee's *Black Unicorn*. See who first published Tanith Lee's book and you will find it is Orbit. Why not, then, send your novel to Orbit? See what Orbit is currently publishing and submit your novel to them if it is appropriate.

Before you do so, you should find out their submissions policy, just as you did with the magazines. *Writers' and Artists' Yearbook* is, again, a valuable resource. If you don't find enough information there, then ring up the publishing house, and ask what their policy is. If they don't accept unsolicited manuscripts, then there's nothing you can do except try another publishing house. Although even in such cases a letter, succinctly describing your work and giving any relevant details about yourself (major prizes, etc!) sometimes works, and they might ask to see at least a synopsis. Some houses like a synopsis and two chapters, others a variation on that. If you can, send it to a named person (whose name, if you didn't already know it, you will have found out by telephoning), otherwise to the submissions editor.

Jane Johnson, Senior Editorial Director at HarperCollins, maintains that readers and writers of fantasy are usually well informed about the publishing world. She tends to receive submissions addressed to her by name, rather than accompanied by the dreaded 'Dear Sir' letter. You are doing yourself no favours sending a 'Dear Sir' letter to a woman editor. An editor may infer, with reason, that you are too lazy to find out her name; that your thinking about feminism and women does not reflect the changes that have taken place over the last thirty years (and that the characters in your fantasy world will therefore hold outmoded views); that you are not familiar with contemporary fantasy writing because you obviously don't subscribe to any of the magazines or go to conventions. If you did do the latter, then you would probably know the editor's name.

Interestingly, where it is now almost unheard of in the big publishing houses for mainstream or literary fiction to be picked out of a 'slush pile' (smaller houses still retain faith and hope in the quality of the manuscripts they are sent), Jane Johnson says that at HarperCollins they have always had good luck with the slush pile. In 1995 one of the two unknowns whose books she contracted was taken from the slush pile.

Agents

There is little doubt that it helps to have an agent. Manuscripts that come through a reputable agent stand a better chance, in my experience, insofar as the expectations are different. Here is a manuscript, thinks the editor, that has already been looked at by a professional person and has been passed as potentially suitable. Indeed some publishing houses say they won't accept unsolicited manuscripts except through an agent.

There are many other advantages to having an agent, such as having negotiations and contracts dealt with on your behalf (although personally I think authors are usually quite capable of doing such things themselves). Perhaps more importantly for some writers the agent acts as a barrier between the writer and the rejection slip. The returned manuscript doesn't thud onto your doormat before breakfast and put you off writing for the whole day. Instead it thuds onto your agent's doormat. That is part of what she gets her commission for.

However, how does a new writer acquire an agent? The answer is: with difficulty. Indeed the difficulty is such that I feel that it is not worth trying. Every writer must expect some rejection slips from publishers, but although everyone knows that, or should know that, it is nonetheless painful and dispiriting to have your work turned down. Why then put yourself through the similar pain of rejections by agents?

Don't despair

Sometimes new writers despair that they will ever catch an editor's attention. If they send their manuscript in, how do they know that anybody has actually looked at it, let alone read it, before it is returned three (or four or five!) months later with a 'sorry, not quite right for our list' message. The fact is that you can't be sure, and all I can say is, carry on writing regardless, push your work into the public arena as much as you can by entering short story competitions or, if you don't write short stories, the awards for unpublished novels. Always keep an eye out for offers of awards and bursaries from your regional Arts Board. And, as a fantasy writer, become part of the lively fantasy and science fiction community. The more often your name appears in print in small magazines, or in lists of runners-up for prizes, the more likely it is that when your manuscript is on its swift journey past the nose of A.N. Editor, A.N. Editor will say, 'Hang on, that's a familiar name, I'll have a closer look at that one.'

And rather than a returned manuscript, instead comes a nice letter to which you will gratefully reply and before you know where you are a contract has been drawn up and despatched to you.

Contracts for short stories

When I was working on my first anthology of original short stories (*Despatches from the Frontiers of the Female Mind*, co-edited with Jen Green), which was a mixture of commissioned stories and submissions for which we had advertised, we sent the contributors a letter of contract which offered them a small fee and a royalty. Making royalty payments to nearly twenty people, at least half of whom seemed to move house within a year of publication of the book, became an administrative chore that I swore never to take on again. (Let alone the headache of doing sums involving dividing by seventeen or eighteen; we really got to know the meaning of the phrase 'long division'!) Standard practice now seems to be a letter of contract from the publishing house that specifies a flat fee, and what rights are being bought for it.

Some publishing houses and most magazines offer a fee based on word length. For fiction the going rate is about £75.00 per 1000 words. However, some, usually smaller, publishing houses offer a fee based on what they can afford as an overall amount. (Fifteen contributors at £200.00 or £250.00 per story soon adds up to quite a sum.) When I am putting together an anthology of new work nowadays, I ensure that the contributors retain the right to resell their story immediately after publication, and that if the publishers sell a story to a magazine before or on publication, then the author of that story receives at least 80% of the fee.

It also seems to me only fair that the contributors should be paid sooner rather than later. This involves negotiating with the publisher, for the publisher, naturally, prefers to pay only on publication. If they pay on publication then they have less long to wait before they recoup the money from sales. The contributors, naturally, would like to be paid as soon as there is a contract for their story. I try for a compromise, and ask the publisher to agree to pay all contributors on acceptance of the manuscript. This is not completely fair, as it effectively penalises contributors who deliver their stories first. They have to wait for the tardy ones before they get paid. However, attempting to get a series of smallish payments out of a publishing house, small or large, at irregular intervals, particularly when these days the accounts departments are in a quite separate division from editorial, would be a waste of everyone's time and temper.

You are not likely to make much money out of a single sale of a story, but on the other hand you can resell it. Once you have had enough stories published you can try for a collection. In the fantasy and science fiction field there are a number of 'Best of ...' anthologies. Themed anthologies are currently fashionable, and many of them include at least some reprints. If you are very cunning and keep your ear to the ground you may manage to sell a single story three times over. Remember, it is up to you to bring your story to the notice of an editor: how will an editor know about it if it is mouldering in a file on top of your desk?

Contracts for novels

While short story contracts are rarely more than a page long, and deal only with the most basic information, contracts for novels are considerably longer. If you don't have an agent, which, as a new writer, you probably won't, it will be up to you to go through any contract you are offered. This can be daunting: phrases like 'author's warranty', 'indemnify the publishers', 'provisions of the Arbitration Act 1950' or the sinister threat to 'procure some other person' can seem terrifying. But there are now various books and guides to help you through a contract, which will explain these strange phrases and demystify them. In *Writers' and Artists' Yearbook* there is a helpful short section by Michael Legat, who has over the years written extensively on contracts and publishing procedure. He recommends that you should at least compare the contract you are offered with a typical Minimum Terms Agreement (which can be found in his books, *An Author's Guide to Publishing* and *Understanding Publishers' Contracts*). The Minimum Terms Agreement was developed by the Society of Authors and the Writers' Guild and is signed by a publishing house on the one hand and the Society and Guild on the other. There is no standard MTA, and publishers have their own variations, but if a publisher accepts the MTA then they are committing themselves to offering terms that are at least as good as those in the MTA.

If you belong to the Society of Authors or the Writers' Guild, then you can get help and advice from them, or if you are not a member (as you may well not yet be) then you can at least buy the Society's *Quick Guide.*

Do at least check with one of the above publications before you sign a contract. While there are some things that may seem obvious to you, such as checking on the size of the advance, or what royalty is being offered (and royalties are covered in the MTA), there are aspects that are less obvious. For example, is the royalty being offered on the published price of your book, or on the price received (in which case the royalty should be higher); have the publishers agreed to pay the royalties owing to you every six months rather than every twelve months; have they agreed to publish your book within a certain time period? What happens to your book if the publisher is bought out by someone else (not an uncommon occurrence these days)? Or if they let your book go out of print?

It is perfectly acceptable to raise any queries you have with your editor, as long as you do so reasonably and politely. No editor is going to be in a hurry to sign you up for book number two if you involved her in a lengthy and vituperative wrangle over the contract for book number one. On the other hand, just because this is going to be your first published novel is no reason for you to be paid annually rather than six monthly! Nor, just because they have been so kind as to take it, does it mean that they can have your next twelve novels on exactly the same terms!

It is in everybody's interests that both sides should be happy with the agreement. If they have accepted your first novel, then the chances are they will want to publish your future work. It is not in their interests to jeopardise future relationships with you. However, there is no denying that the publishers' priorities may not quite tally with yours. And there is no denying that their taste may not tally with yours, particularly over the matter of the cover or jacket, an issue which it seems authors are doomed to be made miserable by.

The advance

The advance is a sum of money that is paid to you against the royalties that you will earn. It can be paid in a variety of stages, often in two instalments, half when you sign the contract and half when the book is published. An advance is precisely that: an advance. It is not a fee. You will earn out your advance through the royalties on the sale of your book. The advance, therefore, will be calculated according to projected sales over the first eighteen months or so. Every publisher, reasonably enough, hopes to recoup as soon as possible the advance paid out.

Ignore all that you have read in the press about huge advances. Every now and again a first-time author gets a massive advance. But this does not happen very often. A first-time author cannot expect to receive an advance that would even buy the time to write the second novel, let alone build a swimming pool. Do not, on any account, tell your boss what you really think of him (or her): the chances of your being able to give up your job before book three or four are very small. Terry Pratchett, for example, did not move to full-time writing until the paperback edition of *Mort* was out, novel number seven, and that was only because at that point he signed a contract that he knew would give him five years' reliable income (interview with Brendan Wignall, *Interzone 51*, Sept 1991)

You are likely to get a smaller advance from a small publishing house that does small print runs than from a house that regularly prints 100,000 copies or more. But size of print run is no indication of literary quality. Nor indeed is the amount of publicity that an author gets.

And what about all my sequels? I hear the passionate fantasy writer cry. What about these three, four and five book deals that I keep on reading about? As Jane Johnson says, at HarperCollins they are happy to commit themselves to a series if they really like the material, whether it is a first novel or a fifth. However, it seems to me sensible to concentrate on the quality of the first book and put your all into that. If the publishers want it and like it, they will ask you to develop it in further books. Brian Jacques was not thinking of trilogies when he sold *Redwall*, as I said earlier . And now the eighth in the series has just been published.

Expectations

As I have said earlier, if you're writing with the sole aim of getting rich quick, then you're on a hiding to nothing. Nonetheless, it is encouraging to know, as you toil at building up the depth and texture of your created world, that there are people, a considerable number of people, out there who are keen buyers of fantasy. But fantasy does not come top of the fastselling list, so if it is instant riches you are after, then you should be looking at romance or crime as more suitable genres. That is, if you can't manage to do a Michael Crichton and provide dinosaurs, skullduggery and a Spielberg tie-in (not to mention a lawyer being eaten up); or, perhaps more surprisingly, turn the history of twentieth-century China into a book that made more money than any paperback had ever done in one year in Britain, as Jung Chang did triumphantly with *Wild Swans* in 1993. It is salutary to look at the annual survey of the hundred highest paperback sellers provided by Alex Hamilton for the *Guardian*, and reproduced in *Writers' and Artists' Yearbook*. In the accompanying article in the *Yearbook*, Alex Hamilton points out the distinction between fastsellers and bestsellers. Bestsellers may start off slowly, and only over the years build up substantial cumulative sales. The fastsellers that he is ranking are limited to paperbacks that have appeared for the first time that particular year from British publishers.

Where did fantasy authors rank in the most recently compiled list, for the year 1994? Top is Terry Pratchett at number 30 with *Men at Arms*, with no other fantasy writers in the top 50. This is comparable to the previous year, when only Terry Pratchett and Douglas Adams featured in the top 50. There's food for thought. At number 55 is David Eddings with *The Shining Ones*, then no more fantasy until Tad Williams' *Siege* at number 89, closely followed by Terry Brooks' *The Talismans of Shannara* at number 91. The previous year books by both David Eddings and Terry Brooks featured in the top 100.

So we find only four fantasy authors in the top fastselling 100. And three of those featured in the previous year's list. The only newcomer to the most recent list is Tad Williams. If you want to be a fastseller, then it seems to help if you have a big name and can produce a book a year.

But then it is the bestseller lists you are aiming for, isn't it? The ones in which quality is revealed over long periods of time (which is not to say that quality doesn't get in to the fast-seller lists too, but it is not a prerequisite). Unfortunately, those long periods of time have been known to last longer than an author's lifetime: I think it is better not to give up the day job yet.

Copyediting and proofreading

You have finished the book to your satisfaction, and to the satisfaction of your editor. You have signed a contract and handed over a manuscript and possibly nowadays a disc. The editor will have the manuscript checked for inconsistencies, apply house style and refer any queries to you. You will next see your book when it is in the stage of page proofs. At this stage you must resist all temptations to rewrite, to 'make it better': put all that energy into your next book instead.

But do read your proofs very very carefully and mark all mistakes clearly in the margins. The correction marks used in correcting proofs are reproduced in *Writers' and Artists' Yearbook*, but don't worry about slavishly following them. Your proof corrections will be collated with the corrections made by a professional proof reader, so the actual marks you use will not be sent back to the printers. What is important is that you pick up all the mistakes.

There is an amusing scene in Muriel Spark's novel *A Far Cry from Kensington* in which nobody manages to correct 'blind man' to what it should be, 'blond man', on the first page of the proofs. As the novel in question is a thriller, the plot is considerably affected by this mistake. All proofreaders and editors have a fund of funny anecdotes of horrifying near-disasters (misspelling an author's name on the jacket is particularly nightmarish), but it is becoming increasingly less funny as the standards of book production, despite all technological advances, are slipping. It seems that almost no publishing house can now be trusted to produce a book that is free of errors.

Of the titles submitted for this year's Tiptree Award, for which I was one of the judges (the Tiptree, set up in memory of the late James Tiptree Jr, is for a work of fantasy or science fiction, full-length or short, that most enlarges our understanding of the concept of gender), there was a first novel published by Millennium of which not only was every page littered with errors, but one of the protagonists appeared as Lara on one page and Laura on the next. It made the novel almost unreadable. This is bad enough in a mainstream novel, but in a fantasy, where names are not always familiar-sounding, it is potentially disastrous. For all the reader knows, Ishwar and Ashwar, or T'rin and T'rir, are not printers' errors, but are separate characters, twins perhaps, or at least from the same family ...

I consider faulty proofreading to be a gross disservice to authors.

It is notoriously difficult to proofread your own work. The author tends to lack the distance that is necessary to read the words as they are, and not as they are imagined. Unfortunately, authors are now apparently obliged, if they want their work to appear error-free, to take on the responsibility themselves.

Self-publishing

Developments over the last five or so years in 'desktop publishing', with increasingly sophisticated software available at moderate prices, has made self-publishing a real possibility. It has also become increasingly attractive to authors who find that the tendency towards merging (or devouring) in the publishing world means that their work is not considered unless it is seen to have reliable potential for sales. The story of Jill Paton Walsh and her novel *Knowledge of Angels* has come to symbolise the story of all authors who are, or consider themselves to be, a bit 'different' – too different for the big publishing houses. *Knowledge of Angels* was turned down by various publishing houses in the UK until finally Jill Paton Walsh published it herself. It was then shortlisted for the Booker Prize and shot to prominence in the ongoing debate about all that is wrong with UK publishing. It received extra publicity as well from the fact that that year was a particularly contentious year in the world of Booker, and one of the judges broke ranks to say that *Knowledge of Angels* should have won rather than the actual winner.

This is a rather unusual tale of self-publishing. For a start, Jill Paton Walsh is an established and highly respected author, although certainly not the only established and respected author to have self-published a novel. Established authors are finding that some publishers are turning down their work if it is too different from work that has been shown to produce reliable sales figures. One wonders if perhaps the fantasy element of *Knowledge of Angels* put off some faint-hearted editors. If you are going in for self-publishing, then being a known name is of course an enormous help in terms of press coverage. And in this instance, the book had already been published in the USA, so the author was not starting from scratch with only a typescript. Nonetheless, to thumb your nose at the publishing establishment and end up on the Booker shortlist is no mean feat, and shows that determination will get you far.

However, self-publishing does require a bit more than determination. It also requires capital: you may be able to handle the design and layout yourself, but you will still have to pay for the book to be printed and bound. A major problem is distribution. With a small print run (which is all you would be able to do) you could sell direct by mail order, but then press coverage, word of mouth recommendation and publicity in general are even more important. If your book is in the bookshop, then, even if customers haven't heard of it, they might at least see it, pick it up, and, if it is sufficiently attractive, buy it. But if you're selling from your sitting room, then whoever is going to buy it must – obviously – have heard of it and know how to get hold of it.

One major advantage of self-publishing is that you know to whom you have sent the review copies, and you can then chase up that journalist or magazine editor yourself. For which you will probably need thick skin and an optimistic outlook on life, but those come free ...

To have your book published conventionally by an ordinary commercial publisher is no guarantee that it will be reviewed. Some authors, I fear, have found that it is no guarantee that review copies of their book are even sent out. And now I will close this chapter with a brief look at publicity, or the lack of it.

Publicity

The amount of publicity that an author gets can be directly related to the amount of money that a publishing house is willing to spend on publicising the book. And that is directly related to the size of the advance. So if instead of being sent around the country first class, you are merely invited to your local bookshop for a signing session, and besides your proud Mum and Dad, your embarrassed teenage children, and the dog, only three people turn up, do not be disheartened. The grinning person in all the colour supplements has not written a better book than you; it is just that the grinning person received a much larger advance than you and the publishers are extremely anxious about getting it back.

Do all you can to help your book. Fill in the questionnaire that your publishers will have sent you, and do not hold back from mentioning all contacts in the press or the book trade that you have.

You have, of course, by writing fantasy, made an excellent choice, for there are large numbers of very enthusiastic readers out there. So the national press ignores you. Well, so what? Do not expect, on publication day, a host of eager readers outside your front door.

Your book has yet to find all its readers. If it is a good book, then it will find them. Don't worry about it. Buy your Mum a bunch of flowers and thank her for being so supportive, and then focus all your attention on your next book.

10
Some last words of encouragement

> When the tale of their journeyings was told, there were other tales, and yet more tales, tales of long ago, and tales of new things, and tales of no time at all, till Bilbo's head fell forward on his chest, and he snored comfortably in a corner. (*The Hobbit*, p.250)

Bilbo's adventures are over and he is on his way home to his hobbit-hole. It is the time for stories now, stories that grow out of his experience, build on it, embellish it, and take off from it, and here, at the house of Elrond in the valley of Rivendell, stories flourish. These are tales of long ago, tales of new things and tales of no time at all. You might think that Bilbo, short, stout and furry-footed, is an unlikely hero, yet after all he is an archetypal hero of fantasy, for his heart is strong and pure. And with the bones of the dragon now crumbled, with the Arkenstone buried deep beneath the Mountain, with Wargs and Goblins vanquished, he surely deserves to rest at last and snore in comfort.

You, however, have work to do. Tales – of long ago, of new things and of no time at all – are waiting to be told.

In the course of this book I have quoted from and referred to a wide range of writers and their work. I hope that I have shown not just how wide-ranging the genre of fantasy is, and how much it encompasses, but also how important a part it plays: in our literature and in our lives. I hope I have given you a glimpse of how it may feed our dreams, and how it may dramatise our fears. Fantasy nurtures and nourishes many different forms of writing, as well as nourishing painting, composing, and indeed all the creative arts.

If you are going to write fantasy, it is a serious and profound commitment that you are making. As you have seen, the writers I have referred to take their commitment seriously, and I am including, of course, those who write comic fantasy.

I cannot tell you how to be a good writer. That is something you must work at for yourself.

I can sum up with some cautionary words and some encouraging words. I shall start with the cautionary words, and do remember, that rules do not always have to be abided by.

A short list of what not to do

Don't try to fool your readers, and don't confuse them.

Don't withhold information that is necessary to the story or plot.

Don't change the rules of your world without letting on. As Lisa Tuttle has said, good magic, like bad, has to have limits, unless you are using God as a character.

Don't confuse quantity with quality. Trilogies are not better than short stories: they are simply longer.

Don't panic.

Don't despair.

A short list of what to do

Do write every day if you possibly can. At the very least sit down at your desk every day.

Do keep a notebook with you at all times. Use it to jot down images, ideas, scraps of overheard conversations, sensations, smells, views. That distant view from the Intercity of a square Saxon tower may fit nicely into your description of what your characters can see as they flee down the rutted cart track ...

Do get your work listened to. Meet up with other writers as often as you can, either informally or at conventions or on writing courses. Ideas feed each other.

Do join the BSFA, or the BFS, or an equivalent organisation if you don't live in Britain.

Do get hold of David Langford's monthly SF and Fantasy newsletter *Ansible*, if only to laugh at Thog's Masterclass and be warned that lazy, slipshod or just plain crazy sentences do not go unnoticed.

Do read as much as you possibly can.

Do write as much as you possibly can.

As I opened this book with a quotation from Ursula K. Le Guin, so I would like to close it by quoting from the same speech. 'Fantasy is true, of course. It isn't factual, but it is true. Children know that. Adults know it too, and that is precisely why many of them are afraid of fantasy. They know that its truth challenges, even threatens, all that is false, all that is phony, unnecessary, and trivial in the life they have let themselves be forced into living. They are afraid of dragons, because they are afraid of freedom.' (*The Language of the Night*, p.36)

Finally, then, do have faith in your endeavour, and the courage to pursue it.

List of works cited in the text

Original publication dates are given in brackets after the title, followed by details of a recent edition, where available and where different from the first edition. Quotations in the text are taken from the latter, except where otherwise stated.

Adams, Douglas, *The Hitch Hiker's Guide to the Galaxy* (BBC Radio Series 1978), Millennium, 1994
  Mostly Harmless (1992), Pan, 1993
Atwood, Margaret, *The Handmaid's Tale* (1986), Virago, 1987
Baum, Frank L., *The Wizard of Oz* (1900), Penguin, 1995
Burroughs, Edgar Rice, *The Land that Time Forgot*, 1924
  Tarzan of the Apes, 1914
Campbell, Ramsey, *Alone With the Horrors*, Headline, 1994
Carroll, Lewis, *Alice's Adventures in Wonderland* and *Through the Looking Glass* (1865 and 1872), Wordsworth, 1993
Carter, Angela, *The Bloody Chamber and other adult tales* (1979), Vintage, 1995
Chambers, Aidan, *The Reluctant Reader*, 1969
Coe, Jonathan, *Oh, What a Carve Up!* (1994), Penguin, 1995
Doyle, Arthur Conan, *The Lost World* (1912), Sutton Classics, 1995
Dunsany, Lord, *A Dreamer's Tales*, 1910
Evans, Christopher, and Holdstock, Robert (eds), *Other Edens*, Unwin, 1987, etc.
Fowler, Karen Joy, 'The Faithful Companion at Forty' in *Letters from Home*, Pat Cadigan, Karen Joy Fowler and Pat Murphy, The Women's Press, 1991
Garner, Alan, *The Weirdstone of Brisingamen* (1960), Lions, 1992
  The Owl Service (1967), Lions, 1992
  Red Shift (1973), Lions, 1992
Green, Jen, and LeFanu, Sarah (eds), *Despatches from the Frontiers of the Female Mind*, The Women's Press, 1985
Haggard, H. Rider, *King Solomon's Mines* (1885), Puffin, 1994
Hambly, Barbara, *The Time of the Dark* (1982), Unwin, 1985
Hendry, Diana, *Harvey Angell* (Julia MacRae, 1991), Red Fox, 1993
  The Awesome Bird, Julia MacRae, 1995
Holdstock, Robert, *Mythago Wood* (Gollancz, 1984), Grafton, 1993
  Lavondyss (Gollancz , 1988), Grafton, 1990
Holt, Tom, *Odds and Gods*, Orbit, 1995

Jacobs, W.W., 'The Monkey's Paw' (1902), in *The Monkey's Paw and other stories*, Robin Clark, 1994

Jacques, Brian, *Redwall* (Hutchinson, 1986), Red Fox, 1991

Jackson, Steve, and Livingstone, Ian, *The Warlock Of Firetop Mountain* and the *Fighting Fantasy* series, Puffin, 1982, etc.

James, M.R., 'Oh, Whistle, and I'll Come to You, My Lad', in *Ghost Stories of an Antiquary*, Edward Arnold, 1904 (quotes in text from *The Ghost Stories of M.R. James*, Edward Arnold, 1931), *Complete Ghost Stories*, Penguin, 1987

Jones, Gwyneth (as Ann Halam), *King Death's Garden*, Orchard, 1986

Kingsley, Charles, *The Water-Babies* (1863), Penguin/Puffin, 1995

Langford, David, *Let's Hear It For the Deaf Man*, NESFA Press, 1992

Lee, Tanith, *Women as Demons*, The Women's Press, 1989
  Black Unicorn (Tor, 1991), Orbit, 1994

Le Guin, Ursula K, *The Language of the Night: Essays on Fantasy and Science Fiction*, revised edition, The Women's Press, 1989 (first published G P Putnam's Sons, 1979);
  Tehanu (Gollancz, 1990), Penguin, 1993;
  The Left Hand of Darkness (1969) , Orbit, 1992

Lewis, C.S., *The Lion, the Witch and the Wardrobe* (1950), Lions, 1992

Moorcock, Michael, *Elric of Melniboné* (Hutchinson, 1972), Grafton, 1989

Murphy, Jill, *The Worst Witch* (1978), Puffin, 1996

Nesbit, Edith, *Five Children and It* (1902), Wordsworth, 1993
  The Treasure Seekers (1899), Puffin, 1995
  The Railway Children (1906), Penguin, 1995

Nicholls, Stan, *Wordsmiths of Wonder*, Orbit, 1993

Palmer, Jane, *The Planet Dweller*, The Women's Press, 1985

Pratchett, Terry, *Sourcery* (Gollancz, 1988), Corgi, 1994
  Wyrd Sisters (Gollancz, 1988), Corgi, 1993
  Small Gods (Gollancz, 1992), Corgi, 1993
  Men At Arms (Gollancz, 1993), Corgi, 1994

Pratchett, Terry and Briggs, Stephen, *The Discworld Companion*, Gollancz, 1994

Rankin, Robert, *The AntiPope* (first in the *Brentford Trilogy*), (Pan, 1981), Corgi, 1991

Rhys, Jean, *Wide Sargasso Sea* (André Deutsch, 1966), Penguin, 1990

Roberts, Michèle, *The Wild Girl*, Methuen, 1984
  Flesh and Blood, Virago, 1994

Ryman, Geoff, *The Warrior Who Carried Life*, Unwin, 1985

Salmonson, Jessica (ed.), *Amazons!*, DAW, 1979

Sellers, Susan (ed.), *Taking Reality By Surprise: Writing for Pleasure and Publication*, The Women's Press, 1991

Spark, Muriel, *A Far Cry From Kensington*, Constable, 1988

Shelley, Mary, *Frankenstein, or the Modern Prometheus* (1818), Penguin, 1994

Swanwick, Michael, *The Iron Dragon's Daughter*, Millennium, 1993

Tolkien, J.R.R. *The Hobbit* (George Allen & Unwin, 1937) (quotes in text from Unwin Hyman anniversary edition, 1987)

Tolkien, J.R.R., *The Lord of the Rings* (George Allen & Unwin, 1954-5), HarperCollins, 1995

Tuttle, Lisa, 'In Jealousy', in *Obsession*, ed. LeFanu, Sarah, and Hayward, Stephen, Serpent's Tail, 1995

  Familiar Spirit, New English Library, 1983

  Gabriel, Severn House, 1987

  (ed.), *Skin of the Soul: new horror stories by women*, The Women's Press, 1990

Walsh, Jill Paton, *Knowledge of Angels* (Green Bay, 1994), Black Swan, 1995

Warner, Marina, *From the Beast to the Blonde: On Fairytales and their Tellers*, Chatto & Windus, 1994

Williams, Tad, *Memory, Sorrow, Thorn* trilogy, Arrow, 1990 on *Caliban's Hour*, Arrow, 1994

Williams, A. Susan, and Jones, Richard Glyn (eds), *The Penguin Book of Modern Fantasy by Women*, Viking, 1995

Windling, Terri (ed.), *The Armless Maiden and Other Tales for Childhood's Survivors*, Tor, 1995

Yolen, Jane, 'A Story Must Be Held' in *Colours of a New Day: Writing for South Africa*, ed. LeFanu, Sarah, and Hayward, Stephen, (Lawrence & Wishart, 1989), Penguin, 1990

Reference

Clark, Margaret, *Writing for Children*, A & C Black, 1993

Legat, Michael, *An Author's Guide to Publishing*, Hale, 1991 *Understanding Publishers' Contracts*, Hale, 1992

Nicholls, Peter (ed.), *The Encyclopedia of Science Fiction*, Granada, 1979; revised and expanded by Clute, John, and Nicholls, Peter (eds), Orbit, 1993

Writers' and Artists' Yearbook, A & C Black

Magazines

Ansible 94 London Road, Reading, Berks RG1 5AU

Interzone, 217 Preston Drove, Brighton BN1 6FL

Isaac Asimov's Science Fiction, Davis Publications Inc., 380 Lexington
    Avenue, New York, NY 10017, USA
Locus PO Box 13305, Oakland, CA 94661, USA
Magazine of Fantasy and Science Fiction, 143 Cream Hill Road,
    W. Cornwall, CT 06796, USA
SF Chronicle, c/o Algol Press, 69 Barry Road, Carnoustie, Angus
    DD7 7QQ
Stand, 179 Wingrove Road, Newcastle upon Tyne NE4 9DA

Organisations

The BSFA (The British Science Fiction Association):
    For details of membership apply to: 60 Bournemouth Road,
    Folkestone, Kent CT19 5AZ
The BFS (The British Fantasy Society):
    For details of membership apply to: 2 Harwood Street, Stockport
    SK4 1JJ

Acknowledgements

The author and publishers would like to thank the following for
permission to quote:

Ramsey Campbell, Margaret Clark, Colin Greenland, Diana Hendry,
Robert Holdstock, Brian Jacques, Jane Johnson, Gwyneth Jones,
Paul Kincaid, David Langford, Tanith Lee, Ursula K. Le Guin, Stan
Nicholls, Terry Pratchett, Lisa Tuttle, Brendan Wignall, Jane Yolen.

Special thanks to: Christopher Collins, Diana Hendry, Michèle
Roberts, Lisa Tuttle.

Index